Directional Loop

...ares

Instrument Panel

Turret

Bollard

Anchor Winch

Galley

Wardroom

Bunks

Table

WRO/H/£2·40

Fly West

Books for young people
by Ivan Southall

FLY WEST

IVAN SOUTHALL

ANGUS & ROBERTSON

Angus & Robertson
London · Sydney · Singapore
Manila

First published by Angus & Robertson (U.K.) Ltd 1974
Copyright © Ivan Southall 1974

ISBN 0 207 13002 7

Made and printed in Great Britain
by Wheaton of Exeter

To Barbara Ker Wilson

NOTE

Years ago in London at the end of the Second World War I wrote the history of my squadron, No. 461 Squadron, Royal Australian Air Force. I have drawn from that history to write a number of books, *They Shall Not Pass Unseen* (1956) was one, *Simon Black in Coastal Command* (1953) was another. Though I have said I would never write another war book I have done just that; once more I have drawn from my squadron history and this book is the result. It is written for young people, I hope from a young man's point of view, though I would not pass for young, even in a crowd, any more. It is my own story, too, in a way I have not wanted to tell that story before.

I.S.

Contents

Glossary

A number of terms have been used in *Fly West* which may be foreign to some readers. To assist these readers the author has prepared a glossary which can be found on page 172.

CHAPTER ONE

Ghosts

The ghosts in a man's past. They do not walk each day with him but once in a while they come for remembering. Once in a while a flying log book falls open.

There is an entry dated 1942. My first assessment as a pupil pilot: *average, somewhat underconfident.*

I remember being lost at a height of twenty feet. Or was it higher than that? I had flown solo only six hours and forty-five minutes at the time. I was approaching to land. I was over the aerodrome. Something was wrong.

A curious sense of motion *displaced* me, a sideways motion I could not understand, that did not belong, that had never occurred when my instructor was there.

How old was I? Twenty-one, barely. Terrified of aeroplanes but adoring them. Fearful of flight but afraid I might fail to make a pilot. Suspecting at heart that in a crisis of courage there would be no courage, that I would stand exposed a coward. That is a heavy load for a lad in wartime.

Lost, yet all the familiar things were there to see, the wide dry plain, the distant hangars of corrugated iron, the wind direction indicator, shaped like a T, laid out conspicuously on the ground to point the way to land, the Tiger Moths on the grass, in the air, everywhere, yet I was lost between earth and sky, unable to go up, unable to get down, unable to think, unable to understand.

Then the bottom fell out of the world and my Tiger Moth

fell through the hole. An awful rending sound. Under-carriage gone. Wing into the ground. A violent feeling of being thrown in an arc as from the end of a chain. Pro-peller bent. Engine stalled. Oh, Lord, I've crashed my aero-plane.

I appear not to be mortally injured but have no con-structive ideas, so sit sadly, a moment removed from tears, sinking into an enormous depression. They'll scrub me now. I'll never be a pilot now. I've failed.

Fire trucks are coming and a crash wagon (I've made their day) and an ambulance with my red-headed instructor hanging to the running-board. He has the look of a desperate man, as if no crime of violence would strain his present mood.

'I'm sorry, sergeant. I'm sorry, sergeant.' What else could I say?

'Have you cut the switches?' says he, with a terrible impatience, as if talking to me is more than he can stand.

'Yes, Yes.'

'Well, get out of there.'

'I'm sorry, I'm sorry.'

'Didn't you see the windsock? Can't you see the wind has changed?'

'What windsock? I landed on the T.'

'*What* windsock? I can see four without turning round. Have you hurt yourself?'

'I don't know.'

'It's a miracle your neck's not snapped in two. Come on, get out of there. Get in the ambulance. Look at my beautiful aeroplane.'

I thought it was my aeroplane.

'*That*'s the ambulance. Over *there*.'

I don't know where I am, really. Apparently I'm walking the wrong way.

'Didn't you see the windsock? Didn't you see the wind-sock? You silly-looking fool. They'll scrub you now.'

'I landed on the T. Honest, sergeant. I landed the way it

was pointing. I never look at the windsocks. They all point different ways. I'd have to land in a curve every time.'

I want to cry on his shoulder and he wants to cry on mine.

There we sit in the ambulance, bouncing over the aerodrome, going to hospital to be pushed and prodded and probed and tested for all sorts of things that couldn't possibly have happened simply from hitting the ground. But I *had* landed where the T was pointing. There was some justice in the world. Someone had forgotten to change it when the wind turned round, so I survived for another day, seeing I hadn't killed myself that time.

A fellow came to talk to us. Stood up on the stage. A Flight Lieutenant navigator home from No 10 Squadron, Royal Australian Air Force, *a living Sunderland man.* Like coming face to face with God.

There he stood above us. Ten thousand miles above us. A hundred thousand miles away. Another kind of species. Another kind of man.

All the way from England, back to Australia; home.

My God, he had flown the Sunderlands, that incredible aeroplane called by the Germans 'The Flying Porcupine'. The one in the Newsreels, the one that Churchill used when he went off somewhere to decide the fate of the world, that beautiful, beautiful aeroplane, the largest operational aeroplane anyone ever saw, the flying-boat supreme of the age, one of the greatest aeroplanes ever made. My God, he had flown the Sunderlands and there he was up on the stage, almost close enough to touch, breathing the very same air.

'You'll not be getting to Sunderlands, lads,' he said, 'unless you're posted direct from Service Flying Training School. It's a very special honour and comes to very few.'

My red-headed instructor said, 'Sunderlands, Southall, for you? Forget it. When the rest of this mob lines up for wings they'll be giving you bicycle wheels.'

We were crossing the Atlantic in a fearful storm and the troopship was rolling from beam to beam. How does it stay in one piece with all that human cargo aboard?

How come you're crossing the Atlantic at all?

Twenty-two years of age, committed to the elements like a cork or a bean or a fleck of spume. All those ancestors working for hundreds of years to send life down to you and it gets treated like it's worth a penny a mile. The food they feed you is not even fit for rendering down, the soap you wash with (I'll *never* forget its name) burns the skin of your hands. Every boy with his little bag of 'comforts' packed by women volunteers (working shoulder to shoulder to a background of martial music) from fourth-grade articles supplied at profit by patriotic manufacturers operating to specially reduced standards for the duration of the war. How much of that stuff you simply have to throw away.

Heading for England. On the way.

The most popular ship in the world, it was one-time called. The *Aquitania*. But in our day its glory has gone. Unless it is glory to go on hanging together with nine thousand mothers' sons aboard in that kind of storm. Nine thousand souls crowded in hammocks lined up in rows one above the other below deck, even below the water line. Nine thousand souls crowded in corridors, nowhere to sit, nowhere to go, too numerous to feed more than twice a day. Forever standing in queues, forever swaying to the roll. Groaning and creaking and shuddering and pitching and plunging and thudding and airless and stinking.

But not a word of serious complaint. You take it. You bear it. You grin. You believe you must if the war is to be won.

Grey day after grey day the great ship rolls on. Dark night after dark night. Hour by hour and minute by minute you silently wait for the deep-down bump. The torpedo bump.

Life-boat drill. What a farce it is. Who would live that long? Who would ever get up to the way-up-deck? Who

4

would ever survive the struggling mass when men cease to be men and become something less?

Twenty times a day you say, but not aloud; *I'm still alive, how can luck like this go on?*

Way down underneath in the depths, in the blackness where dead men drift, the U-boats wait. Oh, we fear the U-boat and the men who man her, sallow, humourless, evil men; predators, killers, merciless men. Like rats in sewers. Like serpents in holes. Cold, cruel men. You can admire the German airman for his courage and dash; you can respect the German soldier for his discipline and guts; but the German submariner is muck. That he might be braver than the rest no one in Hollywood or Ealing or the propaganda ministries of the West would ever suggest. That he might be frightened and human like the rest. That he might not be an arrogant pig. That he might be a mother's blue-eyed son. His sinking, his destruction, his death, is greeted by cheers from the front stalls and the back.

He lurks underneath.

His eyes are slitted, his heart is brass.

My God: one day up on deck, actually up on deck, seas having subsided enough to let us out for a few minutes each, several hundreds simultaneously, up there in air that is fresh and colder than anything you have ever felt, up there seeing that grey-white spinning ocean heaving into humps and hills and ranges of snow-capped mountains, clouds above us low and wind-lashed and icy-blue in rag-like fragments; up there, my God, a white-painted aeroplane, painted like a seagull, R.A.F. roundels, hull like an ocean liner, sculptured like a masterpiece, wings like an eagle's, as graceful as a maiden; *thundering*.

Sunderland.

Come, you serpents. Come, you dragons. Saint George will slay you.

Sunderland.

Look there. Look at it. Everyone cheering. Up there to

care for you. We're alive today and may be living again tomorrow. We've passed the worst of it; we're over the middle of it; that terrible ocean; running homeward to Britain.

Beautiful Sunderland. Beautiful Sunderland. Our elation and our relief rising up to meet it. Could they feel it, those airmen? What an experience.

I have to fly you. I have to fly you. For all sorts of reasons. No negative prediction of an instructor will stop me.

CHAPTER TWO

Family

I have a story to tell.

Oh, what a story I have to tell of the Short Sunderland. Out of memory, out of documents, and out of histories I have written comes this story of men and aeroplanes.

Boys they were, not men really. Not long out of short pants, some of them. Still wearing short pants myself when I was out to work for the first time. Jeans? In those days? Never heard of them. But some went out of school into the Air Force, nothing in between, nothing afterwards. For some, that is all there was of life; they were dead before there was time for anything. Others go on dying because of it, even now.

There was a squadron before I arrived. I did not establish my own. That was left to others eighteen months before. At Plymouth it all began.

1942.

Plymouth Harbour in those days was a busy stretch of water, shipping everywhere, deliberately drab, deliberately grey. Overhead, weaving up there in the grey gales, was the balloon barrage. You've seen pictures of them, I suppose. Great bulbous balloons bigger than double-decker buses billowing overhead with cables below, long cables tethering them to ships or to anchorages on the ground, cables for tearing off the wings of German aeroplanes. They never taught them how to pick friend or foe. Getting down between them wasn't fun all the time; bringing down a

Sunderland onto that harbour was a nerve-racking business
if you weren't sure of the way. Barrage balloons. Did they
ever do what they set out to do, or were they simply one more
terror added to the Australian pilot's days?

That was where 10 Squadron was set down. Plymouth.
There they strutted. There they called the air their own,
except for blasted balloons. Mount Batten was their base.
Not the man; the place. Huts and roads and hangars and
slipways for running the Sunderlands up and down. Sunderlands on the water, moored in rows. Rocking on the swell.
Drifting on the tide. Regal and stately and thrilling a young
man's soul.

April, 1942.

A proud and self-sufficient squadron, jealous of its reputation justly won. A permanent Air Force squadron. *Very pucka
show*. Get a posting to 10 Squadron, boy, and you were
something special—or owned a couple of sheep stations back
home! Like getting a knighthood or the key to the palace
gate. You couldn't mention its name without touching your
hat.

Then disaster struck.

A signal. An order. A categorical do-this-or-else.

Split ranks. Form a new squadron. Become two instead
of one.

The reaction was stupefied shock.

The position in the Atlantic was urgent; it was never
anything else. The future of civilization depended upon the
Atlantic struggle. Everyone was always saying so when a bit
of extra effort was needed; even Churchill was prone to
making mention of it at every opportunity. *Everyone*, except
certain gentlemen in the British Government who held the
purse-strings or owned the Bank of England vault! Getting
money out of these gentlemen was too much for the R.A.F.:
hence Coastal Command flew one of the most extraordinary
collections of aircraft in the world—most of them under-
armed and under-powered and under-ranged and under-

equipped. Even their major weapon, the anti-submarine bomb, was a fizzer. Aircrew kept on complaining that it didn't work. No one seemed to believe them. 'Aim straighter,' they were told, 'you must have missed.' In the first three years of war airmen went on dropping them by the thousand running up a remarkable tally of fish. U-boats, however, were only momentarily inconvenienced. They dusted off the powder-marks, took a couple of aspirin, and went on sinking ships.

10 Squadron declared: 'No. No pilots to spare. No navigators. No. No. If you want to make a new squadron you can't use us.'

Hadn't they heard at Coastal Command Headquarters that this was the Australian squadron, this squadron was a sacred cow, this squadron was composed of dedicated young gentlemen of delicate breeding who would blow their brains out if anyone dared post them anywhere else?

Yes, said Coastal Command Headquarters, we had heard rumours to the effect. Split ranks at once. Form a new squadron. Get on with it, mates.

The air war at sea was the province of the highly trained specialist, a war of nerves, an endurance test, an acquired taste. Aircrews in Bomber Command came and went; twenty-five or thirty missions was as much as the average fellow could survive and as much as was expected of him. There were periods when casualties were appalling. But in Coastal Command there was a different approach, a different philosophy, a curiously held belief that if it took a man longer to attain the required standard of excellence demanded by ocean patrolling, he should be able to handle more of it. So Coastal Command crews flew on and on and on until they vanished into the Atlantic mists, or reached a state of nervous exhaustion, or acquired the incredible sum of eight hundred hours on operational patrol. This could mean, depending upon circumstances, a tour of seventy trips or eighty trips or more, spread over a period of up to two years on constant call.

As a rule, the Australians took their Sunderlands south into the Bay of Biscay or west into the Atlantic. With them were Whitley aircraft and Wellingtons and Hudsons, some Catalinas and a few Lancasters on loan. There were small numbers of Hurricanes, Mosquitoes, Beaufighters and Spitfires—very small numbers indeed—but massed formations of German Junkers 88's lusting for blood.

In those days, no one flew farther or more often than the Sunderlands. Out they went, each aircraft on its own, to the limits of range and endurance, hunting U-boats, escorting convoys, searching for survivors of missing aircraft and sunken ships, lumbering along at a true airspeed of 110 knots although their airspeed indicator registered 125. They had a mystique, a grandeur, a stateliness, a gracefulness entirely their own. No aeroplane ever stirred me more, not the Mosquito, not even the Spitfire.

Training men to fly them took time. Not only was each crewman required to be an airman, he was a seaman also. Not only had he to meet the requirements of the Royal Air Force, but in operations was expected to follow explicitly the procedures of the Royal Navy. Procedures were a fetish. If you failed in an action but obeyed orders and signalled Base in proper sequence you were complimented for your crew drill.

You were required to master the handling of your aircraft on water. The runway was not stationary—it moved around disconcertingly, from side to side and up and down. Taxi-ing from point to point involved tides and currents and winds often thrusting with forces of great complexity at the hull of your machine. You were required to handle it like a boat in tightly restricted areas, but it was not a boat at all; it was more like a huge and wilful rubber ball. You had to master the use of engines and crossed flying controls to manoeuvre on harbours and rivers; you had to stream into the water canvas bags shaped like windsocks, called drogues, to arrest forward motion or tighten emergency turns—and once those drogues were out no man of ordinary strength could get them in again until the boat was at rest and moored. Lose a drogue and you could find yourself driven ashore. You had to bring your aircraft up to its buoy, manoeuvring through other aircraft already moored, in high winds and fast-moving tides, slowly and straight and fully controlled, or those lads up front, sweating in the bows and fishing for cables with a boathook, would be wrenched bodily overboard. The Navy expected you to behave in port as if you were a ship with all a ship's tools, able to go forward or astern or turn in circles or heave-to and give way to 'sail'. Godfathers. They never knew the half of it! Near misses, disasters averted by inches; there wasn't a captain who didn't lose the score. Particularly those who couldn't pick a rowing boat from a model T Ford.

Did Headquarters, Coastal Command, really understand this? Did they *really* know you couldn't wish a flying-boat squadron into existence by sending a signal, by rapping a couple of knuckles, by saying *get on with it and don't mess around*?

Where do you get the ground-staff who know that a flying-boat is not just another aeroplane? Where do you get all the pilots and navigators that 10 Squadron cannot supply? Where do you find the engineers and wireless operators and gunners when the Operational Training Unit can produce only one rookie crew a month? Where do you locate an Australian wing-commander or any Australian officer of high enough rank to take charge when in the entire British Isles there is not one to be found unemployed?

But it was Anzac Day, 1942, a day as good as any to get an idea off the ground. So they called it the Anzac Squadron, No 461, Royal Australian Air Force. And drank a toast to it. And said *God bless it*. And so 10 Squadron gave birth to its only child.

When you're introduced to a man and told, 'This is your captain,' you don't take much notice of the dimples in his cheeks or of the stunning Waaf possessing him by the arm.

Unless you're very new to the game. If you've been around any length of time you see him as the fellow who takes you into the air and puts you back on the water again. You see him as the man whose skill and nerve undoubtedly lie between you and an early death.

That is the mystique of the pilot. In his hands, the power of life and death. That is his privilege and his responsibility and his Cross.

When you regard him you think not of sedate and level flight, but of twists and turns and evasive action. You hope he is temperate in his habits, that he is not seeking solace too often in too much alcohol. You think of German fighter planes and cannon-shells and U-boats on the surface fighting back with all weapons, throwing up as much anti-aircraft fire at point-blank range as a small warship. You think of your pilot in the teeth of all that, flying with coolness, you hope, and self-control and confidence in himself. You do not think of the anxiety neurosis he may be destined to live with for the rest of his life. Neurosis is a word you have not encountered yet. Neuroses belong to another kind of life. If you have that sort of problem now, mate, you keep it under your hat or people will be giving you names like *coward* and branding your records with a rubber stamp, L.M.F.—the brand that says you lack moral fibre.

The captain looks back, judging the feel of each man's palm against his own. . . .

The navigator: the brain, the right-hand man, the fellow without whom you are lost. The fellow who stands in the astrodome, that plastic bubble up on top, to direct evasive action when the German fighters are burning in. No saying who you might meet behind a navigator's wing; a poet, a mathematician, a Rhodes scholar. . . .

The first pilot: in effect the second pilot, the fellow who'll bring you back if the captain is all bloodied and dead, who does a lot of flying and a lot of worrying about the crew (and about himself). . . .

The second pilot: in effect the third pilot, the understudy, the rouseabout, the bottom of the ladder though he is often senior in rank to many others aboard. . . .

The wireless operator mechanic: in charge of radio, senior signals man, can make repairs if too much is not shot away, knows all signals procedures. . . .

The flight engineer: in charge of all mechanical things, monitors engine performance and fuel, can effect mid-flight repairs provided things can be 'got at' from the inside. . . .

The fitter: the engineer's assistant. . . .

The wireless operators, two or three or more: serve also as gunners. . . .

Senior air gunner: in charge of guns, maintains them, tests them, and if humanly possible is a crack shot. In an action you like him to be in the tail turret.

There they are, all of them, all ten or eleven or twelve of them, officers and N.C.O.'s both. Establishing the beginnings. Captain to captain. Crew to crew. All crowded in a little hut near the waterline at Plymouth in working hours—that's twenty-four hours a day—but even in wartime they allow sleep sometimes. When you sleep you are in the bosom of 10 Squadron. No one can pick the difference. You have no identity. You're nothing. There is not even an aeroplane.

Four arrive. Four beautiful white Sunderlands obstinately unserviceable for most of the time.

Halliday arrives. He is an Englishman. They're bolstering up the squadron with R.A.F. men: not enough Australians to go around. In fact, the Englishmen and the Scotsmen and the Irishmen stay right on to the end. But why Halliday? A wing commander? Halliday, *in charge*!

Norman Halliday has not had an operational squadron before; they've been pushing him all over the world from one Headquarters job to another and he has wanted to do more than raise a shine on his pants. This is *something* for him. His excitement is deep and intense. He has a squadron. He is C.O. He is the boss. He is a nice young man with a moustache and a fluffy head of hair and a little cane under his arm. The boys don't like the cane: Australians are not accustomed to that kind of affectation. And this fluffy young man appears to know little about flying-boats.

Which is not his fault.

He wears a worried frown more often than he should because he has made the mistake of believing that Australians resist discipline. The problem is lack of communication. And where that exists problems become greater. There sits Halliday on the solitary pedestal that belongs to the Commanding Officer. He really does strive to be friendly, but strives so strenuously that everything works backwards. He can't rise above his aloneness. The hell of it. An English gentleman in command of a new Australian unit—which doesn't know where it's going anyway.

Down on the slipways the maintenance boys are trying to get those aircraft serviceable. It is *incredible*. If there is trouble in the world they find it. They can invent things that have *never* happened to Sunderlands. They can find faults no one has ever heard of. Guns are not aligned, compasses are not swung; if you fix one thing something else breaks in the meantime. There's never an aircraft ready when a crew is ready. There's nothing but irritation, and a growing conviction that it was a terrible mistake in the first place.

Outside the harbour boom the war goes on. 10 Squadron goes out to it daily. No trouble at all. They hop into their aeroplanes and away they fly. They take off before sunset and come back in the morning when the sun is high. Or go roaring off at dawn and come in again before those barrage balloons blend too deeply with the inky gloom. The war goes on, unmistakeably, and far out over the sea an old twin-engined Whitley gets into serious trouble.

CHAPTER THREE

Dinghy

The Bay of Biscay is the battleground. What stories men have told of the Bay for thousands of years. What piracy and mayhem and murder. What tales of gales and foundering clippers. What galleys and galleons have passed her way. But nothing stranger than the battles of the Second World War.

It's a traffic lane for U-boats leaving the ports of France for the high seas and the home road for going back again. U-boats must pass through the Bay. Come wind, come hell, come high water, they cannot get anywhere unless they pass through the Bay.

They live in places like Bordeaux and La Pallice in stables like racehorses, in pens like prize bulls, shielded massively against the air, beneath slabs of concrete so thick no bomb can yet break through. But they cannot win the war in cages. They can only win the war by functioning at sea.

Out there above the Bay, watching, waiting, searching, constantly patrolling, are the aircraft of Coastal Command. U-boats must breathe. They must surface to let foul air out and fresh air in. If they do not rid themselves of that air their crews die. While they're changing air they're recharging batteries too. Up on the surface they run hard and fast on diesel engines, but when they're down they run slowly and laboriously on battery power. If their batteries are not fully charged they cannot stay down for as long as prudence demands. They must surface by night or by day, no matter when, if air and power run low. That is why Coastal Command sits on top. To keep the U-boats popping up and popping down. With each pop up they make a target. With each pop up or down they use power. Each U-boat Coastal Command keeps out of the Atlantic is a victory for Britain.

Britain can die in the Atlantic. The Old World cannot feed itself fast enough or build its weapons of survival fast enough or produce more fighting men out of nothing. It cannot protect itself without oil. It will never strike back at Germany if the Atlantic 'bridge' breaks. The road to America, the bridge to America, weaves and bends and tortuously stretches and out there in the centre is very weak. Away out there the keen eyes of patrolling airmen scarcely ever see it. They cannot get there in safety, in time to get back. Each ship, each convoy, crosses warily that centre span. Break it, Adolf Hitler, and Britain is yours for the picking. But first, to break it, you must get your U-boats out past Norway in the north and out of France in the south, and over each lane sits Coastal Command in its quaint aircraft; a mere handful of boys who would be happier in college or cracking a bat at a ball. That's all you have against you, Adolf Hitler, a few youths living dangerously on the narrow line where life goes on or death ends all.

The old white Whitley, the one in trouble, had been down to Spain, to patrol that mountainous coastline of odd neutrality along which the U-boats crept to avoid the open waters of the Bay. Flying down there, out of Britain's grey and weary sky, was like coming upon another Age. Bright blue sea. Sun-dried land. *Heat* in the cockpit as if you were lying on the sand. No war over there in Portugal or Spain. No people to be seen. Too far away. What was it like over there not having to walk in the morning to an aeroplane?

The Whitley was a long, lean aircraft; a blueblood I have heard them say; but old, obsolete, inadequate. It looked like a coffin for long lean men and all too often, was.

No one shot it down that day. It went down on its own.
Blew out a cloud of flame and smoke from the engine on the
starboard side and that was bad. You couldn't keep a
Whitley up unless everything was working your way. (They
used to fly them uncomplainingly; who was to *blame*?) Down
went the Whitley, full power on the port side, signalling
SOS, in a smother of foam.

Six young men, wet and cold and scared, came out of the
wreck like ants from a hole. Little yellow dinghy rocking on
the waves. Sea and sky turning dark and grey.

Halliday woke next morning behind the Plymouth boom to
face a Group Headquarters signal. 'Air-sea-rescue,' it read.
'Join Whitley aircraft which has located a dinghy. Land and
recover survivors.'

Halliday scratched his head. Oh, yes; he scratched it
hard. What do you do about a thing like that?

He padded off down to the slipway where the aircraft
position was ridiculous. Every machine the squadron possessed was unserviceable. E* was airworthy—but scarcely
operational. Brand new, not a mark on the paint, not
adequately tested, guns out of alignment, compass not
accurate. But what can you do when they ask?

A mercy flight. As if it *had* to be. How could a man refuse?

Yet how do you commit an inexperienced captain and an
untried crew to the highly hazardous procedure of air-sea-
rescue? In an unserviceable aircraft? You don't. You can't.
You do it yourself.

A flying-boat is not a battleship. Halliday had not been
with boats for long but long enough to have learnt that. A
Sunderland is an aeroplane, with a hull as thin as card,
designed to operate from relatively calm waters and protected harbours. You treat it *gently*, friend, very gently.

A flying-boat committed to the ocean swell is a capricious
and dangerous vehicle. Landing on the ocean is an art, an

* Sunderland E/461

17

art of supreme skill and supreme good fortune. A safe mid-ocean landing in any kind of weather, good or bad, is the mark of the exceptional pilot. Flying-boat pilots in wartime, most of them quickly trained and unseasoned by experience, rarely may be considered to be better than average. A few are good. Very few are exceptional. That seems to be a subtlety Halliday has not grasped in relation to himself though understanding it fully in relation to others. Put him in a landplane and he is a very good pilot indeed. Put him in a flying-boat and any rookie captain about the place can show him a point or two.

He called for volunteers to make up his crew and off he flew, out into the early grey morning, out over the boom towards the loneliness of Biscay in that unserviceable aeroplane. People said things about it afterwards that might not have been fair, but he had a job to do, the squadron's first real job, man-size; the first real responsibility to have come its way. Halliday had to go, had to fly; no choice. The new commanding officer of a new squadron could not possibly have declined to go. What he felt about it himself no one knows.

For four and a half hours on they flew, a little west of south, through an uninhabited world of rain and sunshine and cloud, so vast the sea, so empty. No signposts to point the way. No features to guide you through.

What does a navigator think first time he flies to sea? First time he leaves the land behind for thirteen hours? First time everything 'depends on me'? Gascoigne had the job that day—an experienced man; he needed to be. Compasses not right. Nothing 'settled', not even the crew; a batch of fellows not quite sure who was who.

All the way down into the Bay. What happens if something goes wrong out here? You're so *alone*. The solitude down there on the sea does not bear thinking about. You raise a wall and hide behind it: that happens to other people, it won't happen to you.

Dinghy

How do you die if you're in a dinghy and no one finds you and no one comes and no one is with you to care? Do you die of thirst? Or starve to death? Or become sunstruck and go mad?

What is it like if German fighter planes sweep from the clouds, from all sides, and *sandwich* you? Do you die instantly? Do you know? You build that wall round and round you and hide inside.

There's a Whitley over there! That silhouette like a box, like a long and narrow box. How do they move in it from stem to stern? Wriggle on their bellies through stringers and wires? In the Sunderland you can run or leap or cartwheel or catch a train.

Follow that cab, driver!

After it goes Halliday calling, 'Hey!' After the Whitley. Is it the Whitley shadowing the dinghy? Is it the aircraft they've come to find? Still shadowing the dinghy after all these hours? Have a heart, man. That's beyond any Whitley alive.

One moment they have it, but the next it has gone, in among the clouds and not showing itself again.

If you're flying a Whitley, mate, and an aeroplane comes in view, you don't wait around to find out its team. You get weaving. You melt away.

No dinghy to be seen (they don't come that easy), just a wide-open world of brilliant sunshine and heaving sea and clearing sky. Finding a dinghy is dauntingly difficult, but Halliday *expects* it, never for an instant doubts it. It's a needle in a haystack. A stranger in a crowd. An enormous ocean. A minute rubber boat. That they're ever found at all is a miracle of the age.

Gascoigne plots a square search to spread their eyes, a square on his chart and four courses to fly. Round they go, around their square, how incredibly small the dot they are looking for. Distant marks on the water far away. Ships of some kind. Fishing vessels, Frenchmen or Spaniards or

Germans incognito on patrol? That's the rub. You don't
know. Those airmen in the dinghy could be prisoners-of-war,
the dinghy could be gone, on a make-believe fishing vessel
stowed aboard.

Halliday lumbering on his way round his square, great
white Sunderland so large and so slow, so beautiful up there,
so defenceless she must have seemed if you had not run up
against her on one of her fighting days.

Empty, empty square. Nothing there. Where is that
dinghy? Where does it toss and turn? Six airmen in a little
circle, leg to leg and toe to toe, faces straight and spirits
low? Somewhere does their dinghy spin along upside down?

A freshening wind with white-caps and scattering spume.
Another square for a wider view. Sea down there running
all ways, wind and swell opposed. Nothing down there
right for landing on the sea.

'Second Pilot to Captain.' That was Baird switching on
his microphone. 'The dinghy is dead ahead, sir. Two miles.'

What excitement they could see, a yellow ring of rubber
and waving arms and shouting boys, six of them alive, six
yelling to the skies. But in the aircraft there was a shaft of
strain.

A smoke-float tumbling down into the sea to make its
chemical vapour trail, something to be quickly found no
matter which way they flew. Where the smoke blew there
the dinghy had to be. Where the smoke trailed there the
captain could measure wind direction against the forces
of the sea.

'Captain to all positions. We are about to land.'

Out of the turrets they came, and the wardroom and the
galley, securing bulkheads and hatches behind them and
climbing the companionways to the upper deck, to the
bridge. There they took out the escape hatch from overhead
and checked life-jackets and dinghies following the prescribed
drill, procedures Halliday seemed never to have heard of.
'Hurry on,' he kept saying, 'hurry on.' But his navigator

had to delay him. 'Do things properly,' he warned the crew, 'don't be rushed, they must be done.' Then every man went to his crash position and every man braced.

Halliday climbed three miles from the dinghy. Was he living his landing in advance? As a masterly alighting without a quiver? As a desperate battle against ocean swell and wind? As the thunder of metal rending and seas coming in? Or was he simply impatient to get on with it, not knowing the immensity of the situation he faced?

Gascoigne said, 'Navigator to Captain. Okay for landing. You may go ahead.'

An *eternity* Halliday had waited. It was obvious from the slant of his head. It was strange. They never really knew him and he never knew them.

At five hundred feet he turned in along the line of the swell. It was rough down there and the dinghy was off his bow and here were all the issues of a commanding officer and his squadron under test. He must have known his weaknesses on a Sunderland flight deck—they were not his choice—and he must have known he was required to justify himself in front of an audience not prepared to be impressed. Halliday, so earnestly trying to understand the Australians, had ended up not understanding them in the least. Spoil this landing, make a mess of this approach, and he would be nothing but a joke about the place. Or dead.

His hands were on the move around the cockpit; mixture, pitch and flaps; airspeed, height and the attitude his aircraft was taking up. All the things a pilot does, deliberately, instinctively, or else. With the sea coming up, rushing up, height at forty feet checking the descent, opening the throttles up. The ocean tossing and airspeed sliding back; keel way down underneath feeling like a finger for the touch. A shudder through the airframe and the wheel savagely whipped, port-side float under water almost battering to bits, but Halliday heaved it up with precision and strength and majestically swept into an ocean trough, spray flying, speed falling off, riding buoyantly. Oh yes; beautifully safe and sound and sweet.

No Sunday pilot. Oh, no, sir. This man was a beauty and no one on board missed *that*.

Halliday running in his flaps and revving his engines and turning off.

A voice in the earphones, breathless perhaps, imparting respect. 'Navigator here, sir. I have lost sight of the dinghy, but steer a compass course of two hundred degrees and see what turns up.'

Foam streaming from the windscreen, seas flying high, cracking in the propellers, spraying fantastically out. Halliday with his hands locked to the wheel feeling that maybe his cause was not lost. There was a warmth reaching him, an acceptance, and these Australians before had not given him that.

Gascoigne went up through the open dome, the escape hatch, and sat on the edge of it with spray spattering his face and the dinghy was half-a-mile off pitching and spinning its exuberant crew of six. All that ocean to drift in, all that ocean to die in, but a Sunderland had come.

At a hundred yards there was trouble again. Immense dangers for landplane pilot in a flying-boat.

How did one close the gap? How did one get in there without airscrews slashing men to death? No chance to manoeuvre, no brakes. Many times over he tried only each time to be caught by wind and swung perilously close. There were ways of doing it, but no one had told Halliday, and no one could tell him now, and he could not experiment to find out. Poor Halliday, shifting restlessly in his seat, and the boys in the dinghy less exuberant, looking strained and anxious and wondering what could come next.

It was Baird who came next, the second pilot, stripped to his underpants, crawling out along the treacherous surface of the starboard mainplane behind the whistling props, out towards the wingtip where everything streamed with the foam of the sea and the surface was like a slippery-dip, out there glistening and wet, trailing behind him a rope. Baird wasn't feeling like a hero, but he coiled the line and somehow stood erect with the mainplane lunging underneath and hurled the knotted end of the line as far as he could pitch. Away it went, high and straight, but was not long enough and by yards fell short.

What next? Do you swim to it or what? Through the ocean and those spinning props? But six boys in a dinghy were paddling like men possessed, with paddles and hands and ration packs, closing the gap before wind could carry the Sunderland off.

Baird edged back, so tentatively he went, taking the strain on the line, and inch by inch dragging the dinghy in to the door at the back, far back in the great stern of the Sunderland rearing up, near the towering tail fin and the rear turret at its base, where crewmen were waiting to help them up.

A distinguished operation for the record book.

A commanding officer justifying himself.

A squadron proving it had guts.

But there was more to it than that.

That balloon barrage still weaves high over Plymouth, as if drunken or sick. Grey ships of war nose in and nose out. 10 Squadron goes off to do its daily bit. 461 Squadron bogs down again in the technical stuff.

Lectures every day and training flights every day—when there is an aircraft fit enough to lift off—and new boys are still coming from the troopships with that motherless look, walking in nervously, unsure of themselves, uncertain of the future, scared truculent or scared stiff, *unbelieving* when they view the Sunderlands on the slipway. Nothing could be as big as that.

They lie awake wondering whether they should pinch themselves or call quits. Nothing so big could possibly take off. It must fall in a heap or break its back or run up the beach. It is *appalling* to confront that aircraft on the slip. The tail fin amongst the hangars is like a circus tent. There is a photograph in the mess. Every member of some squadron or other, every man-jack, stacked up on the mainplane simultaneously, at once. If you stepped on the aircraft you flew last month you'd go clean through the surface and hang out the bottom—or break the wing off. How many men on that wing? A hundred? Two hundred? They've just got to be joking. It's just got to be faked.

In the morning they take you down to the pier, one of your new mates, one of the old hands with a whole month's experience, giving you the good oil as he walks.

Down the glistening steps (tread carefully, mate), and take a jump into a lurching dinghy. What happens if you miss your footing? Plop! I should have guessed. That's greasy-looking water. Mighty deep.

Away you chug from the smooth stone walls, oily water heaving, Sunderlands out there lined up in rows, moored to bright little buoys, all swinging in unison on wind or current or tide. Don't look so big now. Sort of settled-down. How much under water? Four feet six, you say.

In under the port-side wing. Duck your head there. *Propellers* you call them? Look like mill-wheels to me. Smell the sea there; sharp and salty and fishy; you don't sort of *fit* that to aeroplanes. Listen to it, lap-lapping there against the side. In under the mainplane, right in to the front door. Watch your footing again. *Yes, by George.* Go down there, mate, and you'd probably get half-chewed. There's always a shark waiting for the new boys. In through the door. Lively there. It's big enough for you.

Holy cow. I mean, holy cow. No one's telling me this is an aeroplane. That I do not believe.

It's got rooms.

You know, rooms with walls, with doors in between. It's got windows and tables and beds. It's got a kitchen, if you please, with a *stove.* It's got a sink. I mean a sink, just like

24

at home. Look, you're having me on, this is one you've got fitted up special for a tease. A lavatory? All I'm used to is a tube.

What are the stairs? You mean they go somewhere? You mean there's another floor upstairs? Like a two-storey house. Gawd.

Now let's get this straight. There's a bow compartment where we come in the door, then there's the wardroom, then there's the galley, then the bomb-room, then another wardroom, all downstairs. And what's this thing up here, up the back end, like a dirty great funnel? You could drive a bus through it. The tail compartment. Yeh, that figures. What about *upstairs*? The bridge, you call it. You mean like on a ship? It's where they do all the work! I should have known. Well, what do they do down here? Don't tell me you've got dancing girls.

What's this with the bucket, with the petrol and the rag? Scrub the decks. You mean *scrub the decks*? YOU MEAN ME! Oh, my gawd. It'll take all day. I thought I was aircrew.

CHAPTER FOUR

Touchdown

The morning of 12 August, 1942, saw Halliday going about his business in the usual way: routine inspections, reading intelligence reports, looking in on the Operations Room while crews were being briefed.

The morning saw him unaware. Some men know these things are near and take precautions. Death can be turned away, out of sight or out of reckoning. There are men who refuse to die until they are ready. There are others who invoke death but death ignores them.

Halliday had a functioning squadron behind him, forty-two sorties flown, not a man lost, not an aeroplane, and not from lack of incident or lack of trying.

He left the Operations Room with a dinghy on his mind; even now, so far removed from him by time, it seems he had the feeling but not the warning. A Wellington had gone down hours before, engine failure or something of the kind, and men were known to have survived it. That was the beginning—an idea of his own or someone's else suggestion. One must not be too emphatic.

He took off in the early afternoon in Sunderland B, an operational boat and fully serviceable, but carrying a capacity load of fuel, ammunition and depth-charges. This was not the ideal arrangement for air-sea-rescue. There was about the operation an imprudent haste as if continuing impulse went on causing things to happen. Ten men went along with Halliday; they seemed to be the pawns of fate with little control over anything. They appear to have been committed to the shape of an action before the scene could be viewed and assessed. They were hell-bent. Even the attack by a German Condor—an Atlantic monster something like themselves—was repelled and dismissed from mind as of no further consequence.

Farther and farther south they flew until at 1915 hours—seven-fifteen in the evening—they reached the position of the survivors as reported. Nothing was to be observed except an angry grey-white sea, swell running high, wind blowing strongly and storm clouds gathering westward.

John Watson was navigator.

'Square search, sir,' he said. 'First course 274 degrees compass.'

'Captain to Navigator. First course 274 compass. Turning.'

Round they went, turning towards the clouds and the blackness and instantly another voice was in the earphones. 'Tail to Captain. A red flare at two miles on the starboard quarter.'

That was superb navigation.

Halliday swung hard to starboard to sight the flare before it vanished and there pitched the dinghy in the pitching grey sea, with another dinghy, an empty dinghy, spinning like a toy a short distance from it.

'Captain to Navigator: signal to Group please; let them know we're landing. Captain to Galley; bomb-doors open; run the bombs out; I'm jettisoning. Captain to Pilot Officer Laurenti; run downstairs with the camera and photograph the dinghy; I'm making a couple of quick circuits.'

Rushed procedures. Bombs went out and were dropped unfused into the ocean. Jettison pipes for fuel were extended and five hundred gallons sprayed into the atmosphere to lighten the aircraft because the Sunderland was too heavy for landing. Laurenti took his pictures but from a distance too great for detail—Halliday didn't swing close enough.

Crewmen vacated their turrets and packed into crash positions in a hurry. Watson prepared his signal to transmit to
Group but had to send it in plain language, a most unwise
decision, but Halliday said there was not the time to code
it. A voice from below called urgently:

'Galley to Captain.'

'What is it, Galley?'

'One depth-charge has not left the racks, sir. Shall I try
to dislodge it?'

'Leave it. I'll not be worrying about a depth-charge. Run
the racks in again. Is everyone on the bridge yet? Are you
standing by for landing?'

Some were in position; others were still rushing from job
to job driven on by the captain's urgency. Are there times
when men are not the masters? Are there times when an
event *will* happen? Laurenti was last up to the bridge, but
came without a life-jacket. Stores were not complete: someone had packed ten jackets instead of the required eleven.

'I don't expect we'll be needing it,' said Halliday and
pulled his throttles off and went down steeply.

A broken ocean, rough and darkly troubled, heaving and
toppling and heaving, white horses spinning. It was impossible, but Halliday did not seem to recognise it.

There he sat, his Sunderland in his hands, lives in his
hands, watching the sea onto his nose, *why, for God's sake,
couldn't he see it?*, riding his controls, watching for the great
gliding wave he hoped to cut with his keel, but up it came
like a flood and hit him below, hit him a terrible blow and
broke his keel, and tossed him into the air floundering. His
wide right hand, taut on the throttles, thrust them forward
and the Sunderland bounded for five hundred yards. He
should never have allowed it back near the surface, he must
have been able to remain airborne, but the second wave
struck him and cracked him wide open and spat him up
again. There hung the Sunderland on its screaming engines,
stalled and shuddering.

It plunged with awful sound and rending. Away went a float torn off from the starboard, down went the wing into the water, round went the boat grinding incredibly through two hundred and forty degrees, bits breaking, foam pillaring upwards, a propeller flying off in pieces, an engine exploding, sea rushing in from everywhere.

A disaster.

Crewmen bruised and shocked and bewildered were coming to life with sea swirling round them, escape hatch jammed above them, nowhere to go, no way out through it, waters flooding in, building up air pressures. They should have opened that escape hatch, the astrodome, before they landed, opened it downwards swinging on hinges; now it was jammed by the twists of impact. Every other way of escape was already inaccessible, though there were men outside; they had got through somehow, out through the bows gaping open, perhaps swimming under water. Three men or four men now, alongside Watson, inside the aircraft, his hands and their hands dragging on the escape hatch, dragging down with total desperation against still mounting pressures. Down it came crashing.

Out they went over the top of Watson, as they had been trained to do, taking from him safety equipment and food packs and signal cartridges. Then they were up there, on the outside, and he was still under them inside the aircraft hearing their urging. 'Come on, John; hurry on, John,' but what was the use of Verey cartridges to anyone without a proper pistol to fire them?

He plunged against pressures and sound and came up with the pistol, but was caught by water and rammed against the hull lining. Water was everywhere, foaming upwards, and Laurenti's face outside was peering downwards into the aircraft with an expression of bewilderment. A sudden pop of air pressure and the escape hatch slammed shut again and up came water over the top of Watson.

'That's that,' said Watson, or something like it, and didn't

see Laurenti with desperate strength break the pressure
seal and plunge bodily back into the sinking aircraft. Watson
had no comprehension of that or anything, until he was
dragged, retching, into the open.

They were on the mainplane, that broad wing, sea already
advancing over it, six men or seven beside a slowly inflating
dinghy. Halliday was one of them, anguished.

Halliday was standing as if riding a cart, looking blankly
for his crew, perhaps counting heads, almost impossible to
accomplish; men were sweeping overboard in ten foot waves
even as he tried to call them. Fuel and oil bubbling, things
breaking apart, a depth-charge down there somewhere.

Where are those heads? Who can find them? There lie a
few, yelling for help, their waving arms rising out of troughs
a hundred yards away. Eleven there once were. Not eleven
any longer.

Into the dinghy went Halliday and Laurenti and a couple
more, Watson half-full of water and still vomiting, Laurenti
not wholly over, one foot still to the surface of the mainplane,
as if reluctant to sever his association. Through that foot he
read the signs. 'She's going,' he said, 'she's sinking.' He came
rolling over into the dinghy and down went the Sunderland.

What of the other heads? Where are they?

No sign of them.

Halliday quietly said, 'I'm awfully sorry about this chaps.'

They had nothing to say to him.

Poor Halliday.

On the dinghy wall, that inflated tube that kept them
floating, a zone of paler colour turned into a bulge of weakening rubber. Larger and thinner it became while they help-
lessly watched it. No power on earth to stop it. No power to
prevent the inevitable.

The dinghy burst, and spilled them out, and nothing was
left but a subsiding yellow tube to cling to.

'I'm awfully sorry—'

They would not look at him. They would not speak to him.

'There's an empty dinghy,' he said. 'Let's go for it. If we can get it we'll be all right. Won't someone try for us?'

A hurtful silence and the restless sea; that was all that Halliday heard until Watson sighed, 'I can swim. I'll get it.'

He had been a lifesaver twelve thousand miles away; a different ocean then and a different need. He slipped off but a hand caught him and he was restrained. 'How can you? You can't. You're not well enough for that.' It was true. True of Watson. True of them all.

'How far do you reckon we'd have to go?'

'A quarter of a mile.'

Halliday's gentle eyes moved on from man to man, appealing without spoken words from man to man. With composure and with dignity. It was a better fate he deserved.

'Come on, chaps,' he said, and edged his way to the dinghy's fractured nose. 'Let's go together. Let's use it like a life-belt. Come on, hang to the sides and paddle. We can't miss this dinghy. It's downwind from here. Come on, let's go.'

They were shocked from all that had occurred. They were vague. They were not really *present*.

Watson thrust himself away, eluding an outstretched arm. 'I'll get it,' he called. 'Follow me.'

Mechanically he swam, like a slow machine. Automatically; unthinking; yet striving to hold to consciousness, to continue the right way. Once, a strange time, the sea lifted him and showed the dinghy spinning in a world of grey water and white spray. *So far away*. No man could swim that far, but Watson fixed its position in his mind and plodded on through the unmarked wilderness. Plodded on through sickness and exhaustion and desperation, hoping for the others to come up behind, to help him on, but no one came, no one answered from anywhere, and there was a rope in his hands.

For a long while the rope remained in his hands: it was a ladder, he thought, and there was a dinghy, but everything was sliding away.

Light was grey. There were stars in it. Stars and greyness and motion and squealing sounds as of rubber. He was crawling inside the dinghy trying to find a paddle. No paddle to be found. What an incredible situation for a fellow to have on his hands: everyone gone. Everyone else dead. That's what it looked like. That's what it felt like. So the sea lifted the dinghy up and there, far off in the gloom another dinghy lifted up, filled with men. The Wellington dinghy. No sign of Sunderland wreckage, no sign of Sunderland men. Nothing but tragedy. Watson was sick again, very sick again.

It was raining. Rain pouring down; spray blowing over him; water inches deep and sloshing round the dinghy; everything in the world invisible. What day was this? The day it all began, or much later? When you fell unconscious how did you measure time if your watch made no sound?

It was difficult being alone.

There was a noise in the night made by a Whitley. Once you had heard a Whitley you always knew. The beat of its engines was up there passing by. It went away and rain came beating heavier and colder and all he could find to cover himself was the valise container out of which the dinghy had emerged like a moth from a cocoon. There was a knife and a distress mast—to be identified by touch—but nothing in the darkness that felt like food.

The night was a very long time. More like days than hours. Rain and cold and lurching motion and the dinghy slowly turning round and round. Round and round. More like days and days of darkness then faintly in the east something grey. Rain stopping, greyness growing, light coming.

Water in the dinghy swishing back and forth, a beaker riding on it. All right for bailing with. Nothing to eat. Water, plenty of that, fourteen tins of it, so he'd not be dying of thirst. Not for a while. But no food. What would it be like to die of hunger? But it wouldn't happen, would it? It couldn't happen. Any moment now someone would come to rescue him and he'd be snug and warm and sitting down to dinner.

He erected the telescopic mast and flew the little red pennant and stood beside the mast learning how to balance. Didn't feel too bad in himself. Not really. Then the swell rose up as if the earth were bending, up and up it carried him, higher and higher, and miles away in the east against the brightness of the day a dinghy appeared. The Wellington men, he supposed. Oh, so very far away. But had Halliday gone? And had nine others gone? Were they buried out there in that huge, fluid grave?

The sun broke through. Sunlight shafts on water, beautifully warm, so Watson took off his clothes and hung them from the mast and draped them over the side and exercised himself to shift the pains. But misery overwhelmed him from time to time. Then he would stand at the mast and search the surrounding seas looking for human life that was never there.

He spread a sodden envelope in the sunshine, precious paper, all that he had, and started reckoning the time and his course by the sun, the climbing sun that made the day hot and healing, all aches going except the hunger ache. Very hungry he became.

The envelope dried and he pencilled his observations on it. Afternoon came and a Bristol Beaufighter came roaring from the north. A marvellous sight. That stubby roaring machine dipping its wings above him, racing round in a circle. It wouldn't be long. They were on the way. Any time now there'd be another Sunderland dropping down from up there, or a launch, perhaps, with raked bow and bristling guns and the Air-Sea-Rescue flag. Soon he'd be safe and not hungry any more. Off went the Beaufighter to where the Wellington survivors were, to circle them, to dip his wings and climb. Up there he stayed for another half-hour: all is well, he seemed to say, just give us a little time.

A second Beaufighter came, to chase the other round and round. Two of them up there now. Fine. Help on the way. Getting closer by the minute. Soon be sitting down to steak and eggs and bread and jam. Except that they didn't come over to Watson any more.

Hey. What about me?

There was a crowd in that dinghy over there but he was all alone.

Hey. Can't you see me here?

Don't you know what it's like to be alone?

Signalling with his handkerchief, in morse and sema-phore. Signalling messages to those airmen up there. 'I'm Australian,' Watson said. I'm not German or anything. I'm on your side. Come on over here. But they turned together into the north and flew off home.

Empty sky. Emptiness everywhere. Lonely sky. Very, very hungry. Being hungry like that was having a pain.

Two Whitleys high in the north! Heading south. A black Whitley and a white Whitley making the homely Whitley sound. The white one for Watson; over it came.

I'm hungry. Are you dropping food for me? You're going to do more than simply fly around. Food for me; that's what you've got up there.

But no food came down. Just round and round like a model aeroplane on a string. Being friendly for a whole hour, but not dropping a crumb.

Getting late. Sun going down. When was the launch going to come? Or when the Sunderland? Halliday would have landed safely today; calmer waters, quieter wind. He came a day too soon. What a shame. The black Whitley heading off for home. Time for the white Whitley also to go.

Suddenly time to go. A great surge of power, throttles thrust wide, the white Whitley shaking from end to end, climbing for cloud.

What's going on?

The poor old white Whitley on the run, three German

Arado float-planes stepped up in echelon coming out of the sun, Watson watching, helpless and stunned.

At four thousand feet, a mile short of cloud, they caught the Whitley sandwiched between their guns. From three sides simultaneously the Arados went in, and there was the Whitley (that coffin for young men) silhouetted in the sky, stark in the sky, tracer shells flaming around it, gunfire savage and prolonged, but it was an Arado that fell away. On to its back, vertically down, plunging for the sea. Did it flatten out again? Did it recover from the dive? Watson didn't know and never learned. Into the cloud went the Whitley, into the safety of the mists, but the Arados followed and their guns had not stopped.

The Whitley reappeared, nose down, travelling very fast, straight down and straight into the sea. Smoke and spray shot five hundred feet high and made a mushroom at the top.

All their lives those young men had lived. Getting born, going to school, growing up. All seven of them. Flying their long skinny aeroplane over the Atlantic. Finding Watson and the mates he didn't know in the Wellington dinghy a couple of miles off. Doing all that, and everything else that added up to making life. But that was that. *Gone.*

The sun set and the sea became restless and the wind rose and the little red pennant flapped at the masthead and the dinghy creaked and being alive was almost as pointless as being dead.

Smoke.

Watson was steadying himself at the mast looking everywhere for the Wellington dinghy hoping to fix its position in his mind for the night. Not a sign of the dinghy. Just smoke.

Smoke was pushing up from the sea into the twilight, standing up on the horizon and blowing on its side as if it were part of a ship. *Which is what it was.* A ship was out there. A destroyer maybe. A trawler maybe. Miles away yet but steaming for Watson directly on course. Couldn't miss.

A beautiful meal. Hot soup. Lovely warm bunk all wrapped up. Hold back the night. Don't let it get dark. Here comes the night—and the wind and the spray and everything rough. No voices out there, hailing. No engine beat. No flares burning brightly into the dark. *No ship going by.*

What happened to the ship?

Was it an illusion? Was it a spirit? Or did it alter course? Oh, that long night.

Engine noises.

Aircraft engine noises roused Watson from dullness. That early grey light was in the east and a German Junkers 88 was creasing through the clouds at fifteen hundred feet. It was dark on the sea. Those airmen probably never guessed that he was there. Then a fog-bank rolled in.

A man already so chilled and stiff and wet and there had to be a fog. No ship to be seen. No Wellington dinghy. Atlantic mist swirling about. Extraordinary silent world somewhere in space. Slopping water and mist and immensity. Wasn't being alone enough?

Wind stirring. Fog blowing away scattering into the light. Great black clouds up there. Why did *they* have to come? Waves standing on end and breaking. Dinghy beginning to toss. Water sloshing over the side and swishing round his feet. Suddenly, like a hand thrust out of the deep, the fin of a shark!

How fragile everything was. How close to the brink balanced life and death. A boat of rubber and a shark like a rasp. He beat at the water with the valise, beat it to foam. Down went the shark, but up again on the other side came the fin. Waters so dark there was nothing else to see.

Go away, shark. Go away. There are enough problems without you. Thrashing at the water, splashing and foaming it with the valise.

No fin. A heaving, unmarked sea. A long time for quietening, for little by little becoming calm.

Drifting north. The Scilly Isles lie up there, somewhere, days away. How many more days could he survive? That was a question for skirting round. How many days more? After all, this was the third; to the people back home behind the Plymouth boom he was dead. Men did not live long in dinghies, in their terrifying insecurity. They fell out or jumped out or died of thirst or hunger or exposure or went mad.

Should he drink? The first drink in three days. The need was real; the need was now. Great weariness was growing, a muscle tiredness, a bone tiredness, a life tiredness. No sign of the Wellington dinghy. Were they already back home, safe in bed? Would they bother now about one lone man? There had to be a limit imposed. Who would care? It was a very big ocean and he was one small man. Seventeen lives lost already and all kinds of aeroplanes. Someone *had* to draw a line and say, 'This is absurd. What are we running round here? Some kind of junket or a war? Let him drown.'

Standing up to the mast, hanging there, balancing there. Sea to the end of the world. Restlessly to the mast, restlessly to the side to lie awhile, back to the mast again. Back and forth by the hour, endlessly turning slowly round, the restless ache of hours.

Something out there was different from before when nothing was there. Trunks of trees? Flagpoles?

There were *masts* on the sea miles away. There were six ships out there, fishermen passing by on their way to somewhere. The jubilation of it. The fear of it. The awful perplexity. Oh, were they Frenchmen or Spaniards fishing for tuna, or were they Germans fishing for prisoners? Was there anyone who could say? Out there were friends? Out there were foes? One or the other there had to be, but how was he to know?

Watson took his pennant down and sat low and when he looked again he was alone.

The third day: weariness growing all the time, sleep

happening like a sickness taking him unawares, sudden
awakenings with water deepening where he sat. Bailing out
with the beaker. Exercising to get blood moving again.
Breathing deeply to get oxygen burning into his lungs.
Falling asleep again. Waking again. Struggling to sharpen
the mind. Was it day or was it night? Sleeping and waking
and bailing and sleeping in a kind of limbo hard to define.

Raging seas and raging wind and raging hunger. It was
morning again. Another day had come. There was a sky that
rained and rained and blew and blew. How could it all be
true? Ragged-edged clouds and ragged-edged waves; the
world spinning like a slow top; spray coming over in showers;
a shuddering, thumping, lurching, teetering dinghy. How
could it float? How could it remain? Bailing out and
trying to shelter from the wind and rigging the valise to make
a sail and putting out the drogue to stop the dinghy from
slewing round. The fourth day. Not an aircraft to be seen.
Not an engine to be heard. Rain and wind and spume. How
long could a man stay sane? A fish swimming round, being
friendly in a way: Watson coaxing that fish, talking to that
fish, trying to catch it with his bare hands; agile fish darting
away. A black day dragging on into a black night, rain pelt-
ing down, a pit of misery deeper than any sea.

The fifth day, alive enough to know, everything cold and
grey, all sorts of pains where his stomach used to be. Water
to bail out, clothes to strip off and wring out and hope to get
dry, but no more rain. Clouds going away, *the sun coming
out*. Oh, the sun coming out to shine. Beautiful sunshine
warmly wrapping his body around, and over the side the
little fish again to talk to. (Where did you come from, fish?
Who are you?)

The fifth day. Another day for surviving or was it the day
to die? How much could a body stand? How long could you
go without food? Beard growing all the time, fat stored up
for years wearing away, belly as flat as it could ever be. Not
even a disc now, marked 'Dinghy', on the great wall map

in the operations room. Who'd be thinking he'd still be alive? Halliday and crew, almost forgotten now. They'd be getting a telegram back home: "John Watson, missing, twelve thousand miles away, we regret to say.'

Lying in the sun, rocking to the sea, lapping sounds and creaking sounds and what is a man to do? On the face of this vast planet *exactly* where am I supposed to be? A man's too small. The odds against it are huge. Who would find a dinghy no bigger than a pea? That's what a dinghy looks like from up there. Like a pea. And the ocean's bigger than the world.

A murmur in the sea. Some kind of noise!

Watson jumping to his feet as if he had been having three meals a day. As if he'd not be caring if the dinghy flipped upside-down.

'HEY. I'M HERE.'

A Beaufighter. Its blunt and bulbous nose. Its singing song of power. Its rocking wings. Do you laugh or do you cry? Do you believe it or beat your knuckles at your brow? A Beaufighter from England far away coming down as if it knew *exactly* where the dinghy had to be?

Watson waving. 'Here I am. It's me.'

All so difficult to understand.

Racing round him in a circle. They knew. They knew. All the way from England and such a busy war, so much fighting to do. How do they find the time for one man lost at sea?

Watson making signals with his handkerchief, spelling out *food*. Beaufighter—for pity's sake—with its Aldis lamp flashing back codes. 'S5', it kept on saying, which didn't make sense at those latitudes on 16th August, 1942. S5? What was that supposed to mean? The size of someone's shoe? When you've been gnawing at a watch-strap for five days you want more than signals out of books of code.

A second Beaufighter in the circuit milling round. *Two* Beaufighters from England for one man lost at sea? But getting back a man is like storming a mountain, it's like taking a town, it's winning a victory. Ships would be coming maybe. Over the horizon destroyers in line maybe. Soon be sitting in the wardroom eating roast beef for tea. Red lights appearing in the east, a fireworks display, someone over there writing a message with stars: 'Over here, too. Come on over here. There's a lot of population on this here bit of sea.' Mightn't have spelt out the words, but the meaning wasn't hard to read. Who was there? Who could it be?

Off went the second Beaufighter, swinging away; down went Watson's Beaufighter, along the side, *three hundred yards to the side*, spilling out a food pack on its way.

'Hey,' Watson cried. 'What am I supposed to do?'

Three hundred yards! On the upwind side! You might as well have dropped it over England, mate, for all the use it is to me.

But the Beaufighter was coming again, making a second run, a hundred yards off on the upwind side, letting go a packet that burst against the sea.

A hundred yards on the upwind side! What's wrong with you fellows? Downwind, don't you know? *Downwind* is where it ought to be. Watson paddling like mad with his bare hands but the wind blew him farther and farther away. Paddling with all the strength he had for as long as he could beat at the water with his hands but he saw nothing of that food pack again. Up went the Beaufighter, rocking his wings, up and away, setting course for home, and Watson fell to the floor of his dinghy in despair. To be so close. To be so far away.

Lying there. The fifth day. There had to be an end soon. This cockle-shell between his body and a wet grave must have almost lived its day. Watson lying there, exhaustion in his veins, struggling to comprehend a confusing world. Aircraft engines *again*. Lockheed Hudsons this time, two of them, up in the sun, one turning east where the other dinghy was, one staying with Watson to cruise up and down with bomb-doors open and a marine marker falling to plant a smoke

trail along the wind. Up and down went the Hudson a few
more times then dived across in front and spilt out a string
of packages joined by ropes. They whipped into the sea,
spattering their splashes, placed exactly right. That fellow
knew what he was about. Out swung the pilot to half-a-mile,
flashing with his signal light, 'Have dropped food,' and
Watson waved in overwhelming relief. All he had to do was
sit tight. All he had to do was drift. All he had to do was
put a hand over the side and pull in the rope.

Drifting downwind, scanning the waters round about;
Hudsons making off, both of them turning north; where is
the rope?

It's got to be there. It's buoyant. It was dropped.

An enormous disbelief was rising in Watson. My God, the
rope was not there. My God, the lot had sunk.

Still the fifth day. How much more anguish could a man
take before he rolled over the side, before he gave up, before
he allowed himself to sleep? How much can a man stand
of solitude and disappointment and defeat? How much
hunger? How much exposure? How much?

So he clung to his little mast and saw the other dinghy only
fifteen hundred yards off. Or imagined he saw it. A crowded
dinghy looking like a conjurer's hat overflowing with heaven
knew what.

He waved and people waved back. Would hallucinations
do that? Would hallucinations wave and then bend their
backs like Polynesians and *paddle* as if they wished to close
the gap?

But Watson was tired to the depths and made a sail of his
clothing and sat back to watch results. Nothing to paddle
with. No strength. Nothing left. Let the wind do the work.
Let it drift. But nothing changed much. They still paddled
fifteen hundred yards off and time made no difference to the
way things looked. So he took the mast down and turned a
section of it into a paddle with a water-tin jammed over the

end and flattened between his knees, using his knees for
hammers. Then paddling; out of somewhere producing the
strength; for five incredible hours following stroke upon
stroke. To be marvelled at, or what?

Still the fifth day.

How far were they apart? Hailing distance, perhaps.
Watson trying to draw breath, trying not to be sick, trying
to make a voice that might be heard more than a few feet
off. Perhaps they were hailing him, but he was not hearing
well. Trying to see their faces, trying to make features out
of smudges. Were they mates? Were they German? Were
they Halliday and his men drifting back from death?

There was a voice on the sea, going across: 'I'm all for the
open air life. How about you?'

Who said that? Was Watson listening to his own voice?
All for the open air life? What would a fellow say next? But
didn't they hear him? It was like a trumpet that voice.

They'd heard. They were getting used to the shock.
'You're *not* an Australian?' someone yelled back.

Was a fellow's accent as bad as that? 'Yeh,' said Watson
with a hoarse kind of shriek. 'Australian. From the Sunderland. Have you seen the others anywhere about?'

Again that pause, across the gap. 'No. Not the others. . . .
We've thought all along. . . . We thought you were German.
We've even got a Verey pistol loaded to ward you off.'

They had *what*? No wonder it had been such a hell of an
effort to catch up. They'd been trying to escape! Did a
fellow look as *wild* as that? R.A.F. uniforms over there. To
whom the many owed so much. R.A.F. uniforms, perhaps,
but that was no Englishman shouting back. His accent, and
Watson's, were of the same ilk. So Watson said, 'Have you
got anything to eat?'

'We could have just that. Are you hungry?'

'Yes. . . .'

They were coming together, closer and closer together, and

the unnatural strength that had sustained Watson across that brutal gap was running out.

It was the Wellington crew. He could see that. Crowded in their little dinghy. Crowded in with ration packs. For five days they had been there, just out of reach. Dinghies bumping together, tying them together; extraordinarily gentle hands from men who had suffered much reached out to Watson and almost lifted him across. They rubbed him down and painted his wounds with antiseptic and wrapped him in a sleeping suit made to keep a man alive in his own heat. He was drinking tomato juice and eating chocolate and biscuits and tablets made of malted milk and someone lit him a cigarette.

Triggs was the captain of the Wellington. 'Call me Allan,' he said. Triggs had come, too, from twelve thousand miles away. For a country with so few people in it, you met them in remarkable places. Engines! Screaming engines! Focke-Wulf 190's, four dropped out of the sky, out of nowhere, all dressed up in black crosses, an incredible shock. In line astern they flashed past only fifty feet up, at three hundred miles an hour or more than that, the supreme fighter aircraft of the *Luftwaffe*. Up they went in line astern to five hundred feet and laid over and peeled off and came again like rockets. You could see their barrel mouths, one behind the other, almost on top. Shock and horror and unbelief. Sights on the dinghies. They couldn't miss. Spellbound survivors, frozen with shock, waiting for shells to tear them apart. Seconds when hearts stopped and all the violence of life was fiercely compressed.

An explosion of relief. Suddenly gone, and rocketing up, four Focke-Wulf 190's dipping their wings in the east, slipstreams shredding the air and pitching the dinghies in the wake.

God. What do you do about that? Where are we, for pity's sake? How far have we drifted? 190's don't fly in the Atlantic. They can't get *that* far out, and then back. Are

43

we running in on France, for pity's sake? Are we about to
end up in a prison camp?

Getting dark and a Beaufighter came down out of the
north-west. You're no match, friend, by yourself, for four
190's. They let him pass. No match for four—*or* for two.
Two 190's scudding past. Talk about a city street, all this
traffic hereabouts. A Sunderland now, alone at last light,
serenely passing over as if this were a very pleasant night.
But Triggs fired no signals and shone no lights.

An unusual night of great fatigue and great expectations
and talking back and forth. Events were not running straight.
Behind whose gate would they sleep tomorrow night? There
were elements, already clear, of a tension building up. There
were elements of a race. There were elements of an enormous
doubt. Had they survived almost a week to be beaten by
fate?

The sixth day, clear horizons, no cloud in sight, summer
sun coming up red, and a Hudson coming down from the
north. Look, man, they said, you're the wrong type of crate.
We want fighter planes, not sitting ducks. Look, man, you
wouldn't stand a hope.

'Go away,' Triggs signalled. Enough lives have been lost.
The 190's will be here, any tick of the clock.

'Go away,' Triggs signalled. You'll be shot to bits. When
men like us in a mess like ours tell you to get out, we say it
because we must.

'Go away.'

But the Hudson signalled back: 'It won't be long now.'

That, man, is a very certain fact! 190's will be coming.
JU 88's will be coming. E-boats will be coming. God alone
knows what must be roaring down the track.

Triggs up to the mast scanning the horizons. Every man
on edge. Every man fearing that death was again close. That
Hudson up there, that glorified passenger crate, not really
adequate when war got rough. Suddenly Triggs yelling with
an elation in his voice: '*A ship is coming!*'

Incredibly, there it was. Bow-wave standing high, a beautiful, slim, sleek launch roaring in at a remarkable rate of knots. All the way from England it had come to pick them up. Half the night long it had been roaring south to pick them up. It and the rest. Four sleek launches, hundreds of yards apart, in line abreast, all the way from England, now closing up.

You cheer when things like that happen. You even sing a bit. And you're not fatigued any more and not frightened any more and you laugh and shake hands and slap each other on the back.

'How are you feeling, boys?'

A booming voice coming over the water.

How are you feeling? You're feeling great.

And the bow-wave subsides as if someone has taken a plug out of it, and the engine-note becomes a burble, and the sea begins to heave, and everywhere around seamen are giving you a call. Cracking jokes.

'You don't look too sick, you chaps.'

'Got any steak up there?'

'Eggs, I reckon. And cocoa. Will you be knocking it back?'

Launches gathering round, dinghies in the middle, Hudson paternally circling tightly over the top. These are the things a man does not forget for the rest of his life. Rope ladders dropping, arms and hands growing to extraordinary lengths to help you up.

'Thanks,' Triggs was saying, 'thanks a lot.'

'Think nothing of it.'

'Thanks,' Watson said.

'The pleasure's ours, believe it or not. . . . What about everyone else? The Sunderland? The Whitley? And was there an Arado—or what?'

'We're all here,' Triggs said. 'Flying Officer Watson from the Sunderland—and us. There's no one else. . . .'

Four launches in line abreast heading for home at full

45

speed, not wasting any time, not messing about. After all, six 190's had been across yesterday at dusk. You didn't argue with Focke-Wulfs. Eggs getting fried, smells of bacon most pronounced. Talk about drool, talk about mop up the dribble from your lips.

Godfathers!

Klaxons blaring. Air attack. Two 190's burning in, everybody's breakfast in a heap. Lockheed Hudson heading west like all hell had been let loose, and due east a German ship, a motor torpedo boat with sunlight behind it, looking stark, pipped at the post. All this excitement's too much. How much can you stand before the top of your head blows off? Triggs up on deck manning the cannon, shooting shells all over the place, Badham his navigator passing the ammunition; how much can you take before you drop? How much can the human mind stand before it gives up? Or does it happen later? Ten years later, say, when you're crossing a street. . . .

The 190's fell back where cannon couldn't reach, four miles back, and suddenly there were nine—four 190's, three Arados, and two Junkers 88's and not a British aircraft in sight. On towards England roared the launches, escorted by the *Luftwaffe*, and eggs went into the pan and there were smells of bacon again, but you're not really with it. You're in two places at once, split between your dinner plate and what those Germans are getting ready to push down your throat. All those things mixed up with six days adrift, six successive days when life and death have been running pretty close. So what's it all about? Eight Beaufighters turning up and circling the ships. Nine German aircraft circling the Beaufighters. All heading for England in a state of truce and no one firing a shot.

An air-sea-rescue classic: that's what it is. Bringing back the last man alive if we all die in the breach.

CHAPTER FIVE

The Ocean of Fear

Back behind the Plymouth boom Halliday's successor was
in command—Lovelock of the R.A.F. It had not taken long
to assess that Halliday would not be coming home. So the
squadron still moved on with an Englishman sitting where
the boss had to be, and the war moved on its course un-
changed. One man fell, another rose. When Halliday's crew
did not return, another moved in. When an aircraft was
written off, another was found. No man was missed for long.
Soon a stranger would take his place at the table and sleep
in his bed. Even his clothing, or some of it, would go back to
anonymity and miles away be issued again. . . .

Men came to serve the squadron in later days who didn't
know Halliday and had never heard his name. Halliday was
in the unknown with his crew, along with all the others who
never again went home.

The routine of operational flying began to settle down.
The squadron played its small part in the plan usually
without knowing what the plan was about. The crews flew
where orders told them to fly, at the height specified, the
speed specified, and for the time specified. For ten or twelve
or fourteen hours or for as long as they could stay in the air.
They didn't worry about why. *Why* was the other man's
problem. Even the enemy was rarely pictured except as a
personal executioner, to be resisted grimly for that reason
alone. The moral issues didn't matter much except in times
of extreme crisis. You couldn't go on living with them every

day. To the limits of your understanding they had been wrestled with years ago when you presented yourself to the Air Force, voluntarily, body and soul.

No 461 became a squadron with a base of its own. East-ward they travelled, to Poole, in Dorset. At Mount Batten they had lived in the shadow of No 10, but at Hamworthy, near Poole, they lived in a wilderness without facilities, hopeless from the start. These things happen. Strange.

Low-lying country it was, slippery and cold, pleasant in its way, but not for flying-boats or their crews. The harbour was small and littered with sandbanks. Someone was always running aground. Moorings stretched over seven miles; spent half your life taxi-ing up and down. Navigational channels were narrow and finding them in the dark drove men mad. Trying to take-off at night had nothing to do with staying alive. Manger blazed the trail. (Freddie was his name.) Thundering down the harbour with an operational overload, darkness everywhere as black as a pit, and Manger lost his way. Something of a miracle that anyone managed to survive. Manger stopped his aircraft fifty yards from a pier of solid stone—but lost his port wing, all of it, and his tailplane. So they gave the idea away and at night stayed home. Getting back late from a daylight patrol was the perfect end to any man's day. Finding the place was like playing a game. Is it here? Or is it there? Are we alighting on the water or driving up a road? And when you're coming home you're red-eyed and tired and aching in every bone. You like things easy when you're coming home.

Looking after the Sunderlands, trying to keep them fit to fly, was a form of punishment with religious undertones. Why wait until you die? Have your Hell now. Go to Poole. Not a hangar to keep the weather out. Not a proper slipway to bring the aircraft up on the ground. No room to park the things for working on them every day. Not enough tools to go around. Trying to make workshops out of houses and poky front rooms. Trying to build scaffolds and shear legs

48

out of bits of railway line. Every time you wanted to change an engine you had to borrow a crane. Every time you did anything new you had to make the tools.

All over the world, the miracle, the British, native and dominion born, fighting a war they didn't lose, with pieces of scrap and lumps of wood and inexhaustible ingenuity.

Winter.

When fighter pilots retired to their bases and put their feet to the stove, Sunderland crews rugged themselves and hardened their resolve and headed for the Atlantic in unheated aircraft to hunt the U-boat whether or not it was there to be found. There were better ways of spending the winter-time, ways less wearing on nerves. You'd fly out blind and come back wondering whether you were growing grey hairs. When your eyes were useless, radar was there to see through cloud—strange patterns they were on the radar screens of that time. Hour after hour in a formless world, shivering from cold (or cold was what you blamed), aircraft pitching everywhere, bleakness and greyness indescribably profound. St Elmo's fire, those unearthly blue flames, playing round engines and guns and aerial wires, terrifying some men no matter how often it occurred. Torrents of rain like slabs of water in the sky. There were times you wondered *why* you did not insist upon staying in bed.

Buls disappeared on such a day. Flew into it and vanished. They heard his S.O.S. and searched for 48 hours through every violence Nature could muster. Eleven aircraft searched: two crashed trying to find their bases when they came off patrol. So Bruce Buls and his crew died, and two more crews died, killed by the violence of the sky.

Against the German man encountered man. Against the elements he was a child. Sunderland pilots could have sought smoother air higher up, but discipline and self-respect forbade it. U-boats were not found ten thousand feet above the weather. You hunted U-boats in the weather, under-

49

neath the cloud, unless the cloud touched the sea. The anti-
U-boat patrol or the convoy escort then became an in-
humanely sustained test of endurance. As Manger knew.

Manger had problems now and then. His was the crew
that shot an Arado down: it hit the sea and bounced and
flew away again. It was Manger whose take-off had gone
wild at Poole. It was Manger who was directed to illuminate
with flares, a formation of German E-boats that the Royal
Navy was stalking to destroy. They sent him to the British
ships in error and Freddie was lucky to survive. A serious
type was Fred. He had a lot to be serious about.

So they sent him to meet a convoy and the weather wasn't
good. Four hundred miles south-westward he tracked into
a solid mass of wet; Kennedy, the man who navigated him,
couldn't even check a wind. From the surface of the sea up
to every height that Manger went, cloud continued in an
endless boiling heap. Stubborn, Fred was; if he was supposed to be escorting a convoy he'd do his level best.

He settled for an altitude of five thousand feet. 'The
weather can't get worse,' he said. 'If we keep going long
enough it'll have to break.' Though the weather man at
briefing time with some solemnity had said, 'There's an
awful lot of clouds, chaps, about half-way to America and
up to thirty thousand feet.' It was not Manger's mistake that
he pressed on. He should never have been sent out.

He was drinking tea in the galley—or cocoa or beef
extract or something like that—and supervising the distribu-
tion of ten more cups. Leaning there trying to relax. Sending
the fellows at present off watch up to the bridge and out to
the turrets with hot drinks for that shattered crew of his who
had almost had enough. Manger was trying to unwind and
stretch his limbs a bit; hours at the controls in conditions
like that frayed any man a bit. Shears and Davenport he had
left up top in the pilots' seats to fly on into the west, Shears
on the left-hand side where Manger himself usually sat. No
tea for Shears, though; couldn't get his hand down to the

cup, couldn't get his hands away from controls that were whipping and bucking as if they were alive and wanted to burst forth. Instruments unreadable, the dials looking frantic. An awful disquiet. A sense of helplessness. Where *were* they, for heaven's sake? What kind of weather was this?

Men moving about the aircraft had to stop, had to cling to spars and stringers and bulkheads or anything rigid that stayed put. How much stress can a Sunderland stand before it breaks up? Manger needed both hands to the spar simply to stand upright. This wouldn't do. It would not. He couldn't leave his pilots to fight with this. Confidence in each other was all very nice, but when things became abnormal the responsibility was *his*. But surely it had to pass. How *could* air be as rough as this? 'I'll take over for a spell,' Manger would say, giving Shears a tap. 'It's pretty rough.' Yes, he'd do that.

But not yet.

An incredible impact shook them as if they had struck something in full flight. The shudder in the aircraft was like a hammer blow to the neck. The nose flicked up and the engines screamed and the Sunderland rose vertically at increasing speed like a runaway lift. Shears and Davenport together, almost startled out of their wits, fought this madness with united effort, jammed the control column forward as far as it would reach, but the boat still went up. Unbelievably up. It couldn't happen. You couldn't fly like this.

Manger, like a man demented, fighting the crushing gravitational pull, dragged his way up the companionway to the bridge and with phenomenal strength, lifted Shears bodily from the seat and threw himself in. But the aircraft would not respond. The nose would not drop. The mainplane was stalled and everything shook violently. The boat still went up at an unbelievable rate of climb and a forward speed of nil. It was a world standing on its end and then it turned over. Upside down. That Sunderland was shaking frantically on its back, under impossible stress, engines coughing and spitting and exploding with sparks, and Manger was in the canopy on his head. Shears floundered off the deck into the roof and, with amazing presence of mind, felt for the throttle levers and kicked them wide open with his feet. Kennedy, scarcely believing his senses, was clutching fiercely at his navigation table but enormous forces broke it off and he landed in the astrodome in a heap, charts and instruments tumbling into his lap. The tail-gunner was thrown against his reflector sight and knocked out. Ammunition pans opened and belts of bullets wove like snakes. In the galley the cook floated to the roof in a sitting position and sat there, shocked, while the labour of hours, the stew in the pot, came up to him in bits. Wardroom bunks sprung open and half-a-dozen parachutes like ghosts burst their packs and flowered with silk; silk blooming everywhere about. And on the bridge the man at the wireless set drifting near the roof reached down an arm and keyed an S.O.S.

At any moment that aircraft had to fall apart and throw their bodies out, but it fell off instead. Off the edge of that monstrous tumbling column of air it fell and at once righted itself, men crashing to the decks, instruments and equipment and everything that could shift crashing with them in incredible disorder. Manger was dumped back into his seat and mastered the Sunderland again, got it level and straight, got airspeed back on the clock, almost miraculously made that machine work as it should. He buckled his belt and plugged in his microphone and said, 'That, I think, was a cu-nim cloud. We're through it. We're out. Navigator, a course for home. Engineer, an inspection please, from stem to stern. All positions, report the state of your health.'

How high were they? Up near Heaven somewhere. And *how* were they? In the kind of mess you'd never describe. Hopeless confusion everywhere. A thousand items once safely stowed, now in total disarray. Dangerous things exposed to view. Acid from batteries eating into cables, a ladder jammed in the controls, explosives rolling round, engine mountings buckled and bodily moved, radio equipment wedged among the depth-charges, the cook's pots and pans underneath the floorboards. How do you go through that sort of thing and stay alive? Fly a Sunderland, young man. Anything else and you'd not be around. But that does not explain the pilot's cup of tea—the one placed by Shears under the captain's seat. *Still there.* Hadn't moved. Still with tea in it for drinking down.

'Navigator to Captain,' Kennedy said, 'we've had a signal from Group. 'Go to Gibraltar, they say. Base is closed. What do they propose we use for fuel? We couldn't make Gibraltar to win a prize.'

So they went home.

That was how life could go for the men in the air whose job it was, theoretically, to attack and sink German submarines. For the men in the submarines it was just as difficult, just as hazardous, just as terrifying at times. They, too, were caught up in events over which, personally, they had little or no control. They, too, had families back home and girls whose warmth they missed with aching and loneliness. (Fifty million lovers, the world over, *separated*.) They, too, many of them, would have been happier in college or kicking a ball around a village green. They weren't supermen. They weren't fiends. They were victims of history, like us all. Perhaps they were more the victims than we were, because evil men controlled their destiny and lied to them as we were never lied to. But we feared the men in the German U-boats—the submarines—and they feared us.

The U-boat, from our viewpoint, was a uniquely dangerous enemy. Nothing less than its complete destruction was our aim, and towards that end we trained continuously, developing techniques and weapons and procedures, convinced that if the war were to be won, the U-boat had to be crushed.

At the beginning, U-boats had been sinking ships very close to British shores, but air attacks with virtually useless weapons delivered from an assortment of antiquated aircraft had yet succeeded in forcing them farther out. This was a scare victory only, but submarine crews found air attacks incredibly unpleasant even when the attacks failed—at the time to the aircrews, it seemed they always failed. Even with a direct hit, the anti-submarine bomb was a puny weapon and years were to pass before scientists were able to give aircrews a fighting and proper chance of meeting their enemy on equal terms. War is a game that men play for keeps; the aim is more than spoiling the other fellow's lunch. In May, 1942, Coastal Command airmen were given the 250-pound torpex-filled depth-charge. In ideal conditions this could split open the best U-boat Germany could build. A direct hit was not required—the object was to secure a very near miss which would produce a massive underwater explosion close to the hull. Hence these weapons were usually dropped from very low level in lines or 'sticks' of six; they would fall from the bomb-racks a split second apart, *ideally* two of the six straddling the conning-tower, the vessel's weakest point.

In practice this was an extremely difficult operation and its effect depended almost entirely upon the accuracy of the pilot's eye. It was a visual attack (a physical and intellectual feat) without the use or aid of instruments, often delivered at sea-level into the face of accurate anti-aircraft defence. Some pilots had the right kind of judgement and some did not. Hundreds of attacks were delivered over the years, but comparatively few 'kills' achieved. More 'kills' might have helped, might have shortened battles, but the continual harassment of U-boats from the air profoundly worried their captains and crews and made their lives an abject misery—the sort of thing, I suppose, that one may count as desirable in time of war.

By the middle of 1942 Coastal Command believed that every U-boat at sea was spotted from the air at least once on each patrol it made. The submariners were shadowed almost everywhere they went, were driven away from convoys, and constantly pursued until they reached the open ocean beyond aircraft range. To be effective at all, the U-boat was forced to hunt outside Coastal Command's frontier and to leave his prey immediately the line was reached.

When in aircraft range and travelling on the surface, the U-boat was trimmed down, with the crew at action stations and four men on the bridge. The men up top could see what was going on; the poor devils below (about forty in number) could see nothing. For them it was the constant agony of waiting for the klaxon blast. Even then no one below knew for certain whether this was merely an alert, or an alarm, or whether depth-charges were already dropping from the sky. Suddenly, the look-outs would be hurling themselves down the conning-tower, hatches would be slamming shut, tanks flooding, planes adjusting, and the boat would dive steeply, bows down, and God alone knew how close that aircraft was or how skilled was the pilot or what was to happen next.

A tremendous, deafening, metallic clang; a sound like the end of the world; a mighty and crushing blow of water against the hull; gauges shattering, lights going out, bits and pieces crashing and clattering to the deck. The incredible shock and fear of it. Fear of suffocation and death by violence and pressure. The claustrophobic fear of being trapped. Could you hear water dripping? Could you smell chlorine? The self-discipline of making no sound or complaint, of maintaining an outward calm that each man may draw strength from the other. Had the hydroplanes and rudder jammed? Had the motors stopped? Was the boat out of control and rearing by the bows? Were the bows breaking the surface and standing up for the airmen to see to attack yet again? Or was the boat plunging steeply, blindly, to greater and greater depths? Anything could have happened. Anything. Even when the depth-charges were not lethal.

And the closer they fell the greater the shock, the more terrifying the confusion. And so each attack seemed worse than the last. And when was the next to be? Living was a nightmare. Only going home was coming alive. And over home hung the shadow of going away again. Was this how man was meant to be? Some say it is.

So the U-boats left the shores of Britain for the open sea. Too nerve-racking in there, close to land. (You couldn't go on taking those attacks and remain sane; you couldn't remain in command of yourself.) So aircraft hunted with new instruments, with radar, with many developing kinds of radar, and U-boats countered with instruments of detection that told them when radar beams were reflecting from them. It was a war of nerves and technology and cat-and-mouse.

They did not always crash-dive to the blackness of the depths. Sometimes they chose to fight in the light with heavy machine-guns and multiple-firing cannon. Trying to get in close enough to depth-charge a U-boat, flying an aircraft bigger than a house, trying to get down to fifty feet from the surface with shells exploding in your face—not easy. You had to get down to fifty feet to aim your depth-charges with accuracy, had to aim them yourself, had to press the bomb-button with the thumb of your right hand, had to fly evasive action with rhythm and violence and precision, and (by 1944) had even to fire the machine-guns, the four of them installed in the nose, the button under your other thumb. Was it, perhaps, too much for one man in a huge aircraft with ten other crew members for the moment standing by? Every other man a spectator unless the gun in his hands could be brought to bear on the target, unless he could snatch a quick shot at that target seen only momentarily here and there, thrown by the pilot's evasive action apparently to every corner of sea and sky.

Before he began operational flying each captain dropped hundreds of practice-bombs on targets of various kinds and continued to practice throughout his long operational tour. Some pilots had a remarkable flair for it and enjoyed the game; like shooting for goal or potting the red, their errors averaging only a few feet over hundreds of tries. Other pilots consistently missed by streets and during an actual U-boat attack against real shells and real Germans even the Crack-shot Charlies could make a proper mess. Pilots ready to swear they had straddled their targets amidships learnt from the camera triggered automatically when the depth-charges fell that they had stirred up the fish hundreds or yards from where the target had been. Each squadron flew thousands of operational sorties; each squadron managed to sink a few U-boats, six or seven, perhaps, over the years. If you found a U-boat, you most desperately tried to destroy it. Generally, like the fisherman's fantasy, it got away.

Something about the U-boat stirred up passions. The ordinary 'man-in-the-street' saw it as stealthy, cowardly, cruel and vicious, and there is no doubt it was a most effective and dangerous foe, particularly after Admiral Doenitz became Supreme Commander of the Germany Navy and subordinated all other naval requirements to those of his U-boat flotillas. The Big Three regarded it as of critical importance; at Casablanca, Churchill, Roosevelt and Stalin laid down that the defeat of the U-boat should be the first charge on the combined resources of the Allies.

U-boat commanders and their crews were depicted in Allied propaganda as evil-smiling men indelibly stained with the blood of the innocent, whereas the crews of British and American submarines were portrayed as clean-limbed, clean-living heroes. It was simply a matter of terminology—if you called a ship that moved under the sea a submarine it was acceptable in polite society; if you called it a U-boat it came straight out of Hell with devils at the periscope.

During the spring of 1943 the U-boat arm made its supreme effort. Great numbers were at sea, more than a hundred vessels, patrolling in packs, travelling in company for mutual support and strategic deployment. Where once they patrolled alone now they patrolled in dozens and were arrayed to cut the main shipping lanes between North America and Britain, over which came the essential supplies of survival. The U-boats ran very close to victory, all but winning the war at sea for Hitler in three shattering months when they sank a million and a quarter tons of shipping and almost tore the convoy system beyond continuance. That system, with its roots in history and immensely improved by experience, was the foundation of defensive warfare on broad oceans. Merchant ships sailed together in company, in large numbers, in precise but changing formation, escorted by warships constantly on patrol through the lanes and around the perimeters. Experience had proved it was by far the safest and most effective method of defence for ships at sea; even slow vessels were not unduly endangered—the units of a convoy were matched for performance and moved in their own kind of company.

But suddenly convoy after convoy was cut to pieces. U-boats were all but everywhere, attacking simultaneously from many directions, so numerous it was impossible for naval escort ships to handle them.

This was at its worst outside the range of aircraft and perilously complicated by the dramatic failure of British radar. German science, for the first time with full effectiveness, had cracked the secret frequencies and devised search receivers that listened-in to radar transmissions. U-boats could now tune in and hear the approach of hostile aircraft. Instead of helping airmen to find their targets, radar became a powerful signal, a beacon, a warning sign as unsubtle as a police siren. Every time U-boat crews heard that signal they crash-dived and airmen found nothing.

The whole structure of the war against the U-boats started tottering. Everything went wrong. Nothing would go right. And this came on top of a winter as violent and as savage as any in living memory when losses of ships at sea due to weather alone had reached alarming, almost demoralising proportions. Luck was always a part of it, the give and take of chance, but luck was going the Nazi way entirely and in 'high places' there were grave fears that the British war effort was collapsing.

In terms of human life and suffering it is still difficult, fully, to picture its meaning. Across that bitter ocean, for months on end, while those disastrous battles were continuing, little men in large numbers died by violence and privation, by fire and water, by thirst and starvation, by exposure and desperation in life-boats and rubber dinghies and on ragged lumps of wreckage. Boys and men dying in the Atlantic trying to bring material things to Britain, while all over the world girls and women lost their love from their lives forever. Terrible days. Terrible times. The ocean of fear is a good name for it.

That was the year I crossed it, as a pawn, as an expendable piece of human baggage (neither valuable nor not-valuable), as one of nine thousand on that stinking old troopship with sewage swilling in the corridors, overflow from waste-disposal systems so grossly overladen they ceased to function.

No 461 Squadron, the group of men and aeroplanes whose exploits this book is built on, were not significantly useful, at that time, to anyone. Poole Harbour immobilized them. The arrival of an Australian commanding officer, Desmond Douglas, made not the slightest difference. The harbour was too small, the maintenance problems too large, the men, generally, too discouraged by the constant disappointments of failing to keep flying-boats serviceable. There was one cure only, a drastic one, and Coastal Command administered it. 'Pack up,' they said. 'This no longer amuses us. Get out of the place. Get yourselves to Pembroke Dock and we'll see what difference that makes.'

Pembroke Dock was a pre-war flying-boat base with all facilities, closer by an hour to the patrol area. Away out on

the western extremity of Wales, there it lay, at the inland
end of Milford Haven, a beautiful, long and narrow inlet
of deep waters, protected on all sides, one of the finest
harbours in Europe. There the squadron flowered almost
overnight. From there it flew its most noteworthy operations
and assumed a manly share of the remarkable effort that
stopped the U-boats in the Atlantic. From the 'brink of
disaster' the convoy system rallied. Looking back it would
seem that in the hour, literally in the *hour* of their incredible
triumph, the submarines lost faith, or else had extended
their effort to the point of exhaustion and withered. In one
month, May 1943, forty-three U-boats were sunk.

From the Allied viewpoint everything that had been
going wrong suddenly reverted. Every arm of the anti-
U-boat forces produced its greatest effort and its greatest
result out of the hour of failure—a desperate victory achieved
with a unity and a will that must have shaken Germany. Not
the least remarkable was the coming of the new ten-centi-
metre radar out of the laboratories at the moment most
needed: designed, developed, manufactured and installed
in Allied aircraft and ships without the Germans effectively
learning of its existence. This one weapon, more than any
other, enabled men to find their targets again and to sink
them. In the months that followed, the U-boat flotillas
repeatedly came back with more armament and new tactics.
A battle lost was swept under the carpet. A battle won was
the beginning of another. There are history books to tell
you. The relating of the value of human life to it becomes
very difficult. Perhaps life is, after all, the most expendable
commodity in the military manual.

You went where *they* sent you and you tried to do what
was expected of you, tried to obey orders, tried to be brave,
tried to 'reflect credit' on your origins.

'You're Australian. Remember the Anzac tradition. Don't
let the team regret you.'

'Remember you're British. . . .'

'Remember you're American. . . .'

In moments of vision the Right was obvious, Belief was certain, Truth was shining. God was on your side and the Nazi philosophy was evil. It was good to be British or American. The world was our responsibility for rehabilitation. We believed it implicitly and I am still not prepared to say we were grossly misinformed.

What of German youth? Did they have the same faith and the same certainty as the months became years? Do you go on believing or does your heart beat empty, beat cold? When that happens life becomes grim.

The struggle for personal survival became increasingly dour. No matter what you were, German or American or British, the writing was on the wall. *Wanted dead or alive. Preferably dead. You.*

More and more German fighters in large formations were appearing in the Bay. Twenty to one the odds, sometimes. Junkers 88's as a rule, a fine aircraft, long range, armed with cannon commanding three times the effective range of a Sunderland's ·303's and faster in level flight than a Sunderland by hundreds of miles an hour.

More and more Sunderlands and Wellingtons and Whitleys were failing to return. The sharks were getting fat down the Bay.

Staying alive. My God, it's an urgent matter when the blood is young in your veins. You haven't fathered a child; you've left no seed. If you don't go on staying alive there is no world. If you don't keep on bringing your consciousness to it nothing is there—no joy, no sorrow, no love, no sacrifice. This is the only certainty seen from where a young man stands—to go on staying alive if the world is not to disappear.

If you put on a uniform, if *they* give you a gun or a ship or an aeroplane, you don't stop suddenly wishing to be alive, you don't overcome suddenly the oblivion fear. You are not suddenly made of steel. You remain the same. You remain the boy who wants to go on staying alive to be with that girl, the one who's going to make children with you. The boy then of many years ago and the modern boy of now— just the same, the same longing, the same fear.

CHAPTER SIX

The Luck of War

Bill Dods was an unlucky man. Perhaps there was no reason why fortune should have smiled upon him, war being what it was. It had no favourites. It picked off the good and the not-so-good with indifference and any man who fought his war from the pilot's seat or turret of an aircraft was half-way to the grave before he began. Fate didn't need to push hard to topple him over the edge. It was not that aircraft were notably primitive or inferior; too many things were against you. The enemy was against you with everything he could bring to bear. Nature was against you. Time was against you. Time, particularly. You were placed in command of machines and situations of great complexity long before you were properly equipped, emotionally or technically, to cope with them. Half of us had never even driven a motor-car. How many of us died simply trying to learn to fly in worn-out, clapped-out, obsolete aeroplanes? How many of us were placed in situations of the gravest danger, demanding airmanship of the highest order, before we knew what airmanship was about? The oldest of us, the most experienced and skilful of us, could not have held down a job today on a second-rate airline. We didn't have the *hours*. Hadn't had the *time*. With a thousand hours in our flying log books we were senior men, we were the ultimate authorities to whom the experts looked for advice. We were uncommonly lucky still to be alive.

Bill Dods was a captain, undistinguished by high rank

or incredible deeds of derring-do. He was never decorated for anything. Never got around to making a U-boat attack (never got close enough to one while he was in command); never, to my knowledge, shot an enemy aircraft down (was never close enough to one as far as I can see); Bill Dods was one of those fellows who always arrived on the scene, his Sunderland shaking with eagerness from stem to stern, just as the death-and-glory boys packed it in and went home. Yet Bill had his problems from time to time.

Back in the depths of winter he took off one morning at three to look for the survivors of an aircraft which had been shot down. Three hours out from home his starboard engine blew up. Cowlings crashed against the mainplane. Sparks, smoke, fire and bits of metal flew in all directions—a magnificent and terrifying display in the middle of the night. Of all the engine failures, and there were plenty in the log books of Sunderland aircrews, few were more spectacular than that one.

Engine-trouble was a recurring sickness. Like a lot of other things that made the game interesting, it came in cycles. Used to set in like a disease. Flight after flight, BANG. It could go on for weeks until even a slamming door was more than you could stand. Then the disease would go away, the wounds would heal, and for a month or more every engine you had anything to do with would sing like a bird.

A dead engine was depressing company in any sort of weather in any sort of aeroplane. On a single-engined aeroplane it was devastating. Even on a Sunderland (where one could be pardoned for assuming there were engines to spare) it could be embarrassingly difficult: the aircraft under that kind of stress turned out to be strikingly underpowered. When carrying an operational overload the Sunderland in those days needed all four engines working hard all of the time. Between the lot of them those engines didn't amount to much more than four thousand horse-power. Failure of any one unit was something like being sentenced to death, suddenly, on a wet grey dawn. (Failure of two units still doesn't bear writing about.) That sea down there was wide and deep and huge and we didn't carry parachutes for baling out with any more. What use were parachutes over the ocean? In winter you froze to death in ten minutes anyway. Better to stick with your aircraft and make its fate your own. If you baled out you drowned. Even if you ditched you probably drowned, but at least you didn't die alone.

So there was Bill Dods, on a black winter's morning, with an engine blowing out like a bomb, with tongues of fire threatening to ignite fuel and oil and turn his flying-boat into a blazing barn. Because he had to *jettison* fuel, eight hundred gallons of it, as quickly as he could let it go, and he had to pray it didn't ignite. The enormous weight of that fuel was weight he had to unload as he turned his aircraft round and headed for home. Depth-charges he had to get rid of, too. One ton, dead weight, of depth-charges; down they went into the sea. Down went the Sunderland also. Three thousand feet down before Dods was able to arrest its descent. There, a few hundred feet above the surface, he managed to hold the Sunderland in balance between the power it could produce and the weight it was compelled to support, a very delicate balance indeed.

The heat in the crippled engine increased as minutes turned into agonizing hours. Three hours they had flown out with the wind behind them; almost four hours they would need to get home. But they didn't make it. Hotter and hotter that engine became. White-hot it became, and melting, with masses of sparks scattering across the mainplane into deep blackness astern. White-hot and exploding; out it blew a second time, sheets of flame and great lumps of glowing metal blazed in the sky and holding his height now was something Dods couldn't do. Down they went closer and closer to the sea, but coming up on their bow was the rotating beam of a lighthouse on the south coast of England. They'd never get home, but England was there.

Down Dods went, feeling in fear for the sea, feeling for it
with the Sunderland's keel, dazzled by sparks and white-hot
metal and flame. How high was the sea; how rough was it;
in what direction did the wind blow? Twenty-seven S.O.S.
signals the wireless operator keyed in the last feet before
Dods hit the sea while the first pilot held his head out in the
tearing slipstream yelling into his microphone, 'I see it. The
sea. It's there. Ten feet. Five feet. *Now!*'

Dods thumped his aircraft down and held it there straight
and level, safe and reasonably sound, and any man who has
ever flown a Sunderland will take off his hat to that one. He
mightn't have saved the crew he went out to look for, but he
certainly saved his own.

He tried another air-sea-rescue a month or two later on.
Brought in a destroyer, eventually, to pick the survivors up,
after twice failing to alight upon a deceptively calm stretch
of sea which at close quarters turned out to be a treacherous
swell. Dods was not a hot-headed man; he was a competent
pilot who flew with his brains as well as his hands and feet.
There were plenty like him. Men of his kind were the
anchors of every squadron. You became accustomed to their
being around. They were the unspectacular, solid men who
would survive the war and build the peace. They always
seemed to be older than you were yourself. Some acquired
the stature of father-figures, somehow aged, somehow dig-
nified by events. Dods was markedly older than most, thirty-
three years, a pilot by act of deliberate choice, having earlier
resigned a commission and gone back to the ranks for aircrew training.

He was a logical choice to accompany Flying Officer
Gipps on his 'proving' flight. Gipps was expected shortly
to be taking a crew but first had to convince the experienced
men about the place that he was able to assume the respon-
sibilities. So off Gipps went one April morning to patrol the
Bay of Biscay, acting out the part of Captain with a 'borrowed' crew. Dods was there to keep an eye on everything

and to take over if things got desperate. An air marshal (they thought of him as elderly, but surely he could not have been) went along for the ride and got the sort of ride that came but rarely, while Dods had to suffer the irony of sitting back as a spectator to watch a novice captain, on his first flight, go charging headlong into action.

Five hours they flew that morning before they broke clear of fog. Out they came through the edges of it with streamers spinning astern to an excited call from the gunner on watch in the nose. *Dead ahead, a U-boat, at nine miles!* In a year of ranging the seas the squadron had seen U-boats only twice before. Searching for a whole year and only twice managing to attack before. Now, for their startled eyes, the third at nine miles!

Poor Dods. Stunned was the word. Hundreds of hours he had flown never to be given the chance that came to Gipps first time round.

Gipps pushed everything 'flat to the floor'. Throttles wide, control column forward, everyone rushing to prepare. But nine miles was almost four minutes of flying time, all the time the U-boat needed to slam the hatches shut and go down to leave a swirl behind. Over that swirl the frustrated airmen laid a pattern of marine markers and smoke floats and resumed patrol.

But it was one of *those* days when strange events were abroad. Another Sunderland, F of 10 Squadron, sighted the marine markers from a distance of several miles and turned in as Gipps flew away. Gerrard, captain of F/10, brought his aircraft over the top at the moment the feather of a periscope wake appeared. He stared, astonished, too close and too high, but more was to happen to complete his surprise. Up came the U-boat, all of it, all 740 tons of it, blue-black and shining, directly underneath, spilling rivers from its beams, like something out of a wild and impossible dream. U-boats *never* re-surfaced after having been sighted and scared down. U-boats *never* crash-dived to escape from aircraft to come up again so soon, as if simply breathing out and breathing in. But the commander of U-119, for whatever reason, did exactly that by design. U-boat commanders would stop down an hour or two hours or more to get away from where the marine markers were, to wait until airmen lost patience or ran short of fuel. But U-119 broke the rules.

Gerrard, wrong-footed by his surprise, swung his aircraft away and madly prepared, cutting away his excess height, flashing his sighting signal to Base, running out his depth-charges, and diving steeply to attack. In truth, he wasted not a moment, yet there still was time for the U-boat crew to man the guns and throw up an explosive wall of fire, to score hits on F/10 on both wings and the port inner engine. But Gerrard got through and straddled his target with six depth-charges a short distance behind the conning-tower. Almost immediately the U-boat began to lose oil and pour smoke, but not for an instant did it cease fire. As Gerrard pulled away to manoeuvre for position to make his second attack flak followed him, bursting all around, and into that same flak came Gipps at maximum permissible diving speed, 200 knots, with Dods beside him in a sweat, somehow keeping his hands off the wheel, somehow accepting the incredible, that Gipps, the novice, was flying this machine and handling this attack with finesse and flair. In went Gipps at full power across the U-boat's bow, his own gunners mowing down the U-boat gunners, his six depth-charges erupting in pillars of foam, dead German gunners being swept overboard to wallow in that disturbed sea, in the scum of explosives and a film of oil, bodies of no further use, destroyed by foe and abandoned by friend.

Stationary, that U-boat was. Not a living man to be seen. Decks bare. Conning-tower empty. Then it went down as if sinking, heavily sinking, at once to reappear steeply by the stern before vanishing in the midst of a violent spume of foam.

68

Round and round that spot the aircraft flew, the two Sunderlands, the twenty-three airmen, waiting; each turret in its turn bringing its guns to bear, each captain with his two depth-charges still ready to add to the terror down there. Round and round they flew rejoicing in their victory. Then, from a point two hundred feet ahead of where the stern had disappeared, a series of large air bubbles burst, churning the sunlit sea into vivid green and ultramarine, bubbling and boiling, until the disturbance was eighty yards long and that U-boat crew *must* have been at the climax of despair, trying to blow the tanks, trying to get back to the surface, trying to get back up to abandon ship that at least a few might survive. But the tormented U-boat did not reappear and the disturbance died and the sea calmed with scum and oil where the smoke of the marine markers quietly curled and lifeless bodies floated untended, life-jackets supporting them. . . .

Dods and Gipps and Gerrard went jubilantly home, Dods perhaps a little wryly, but that was the luck of war. Yet it was a strange day (I said that before); U-119 also went home, perhaps not with the same jubilation, but with numbed gratitude for the genius of construction and design that had produced a vessel capable of withstanding such violently destructive pressures. Or was that, too, the luck of war? Back to port they went to be repaired, back home to their villages and towns to rest and renew their nerves, then out again into the Bay of Biscay a few weeks later on. There they met H.M.S. *Starling* of the Second Escort Group, a frigate of no mean reputation in the Second World War. *Starling* got the measure of U-119 and sent it to the bottom of the sea, all hands going down. So the luck of war ebbed and flowed; one week it was the other fellow's, the next week it was yours. Life didn't count for much unless it was your own, no matter what the chaplains or the propagandists declared.

Bill Dods ended an era at about that time. He made a

decision and it provoked a change of mind. Coastal Command said: 'This is the finish. Sunderlands are not ocean-going vessels and no pilot, for whatever motive, will attempt to prove it or disprove it another time.'

Half-past four it was, on the afternoon of that moment of truth, and Sunderland O/461 found a yellow rubber dinghy with six men aboard. Survivors of a Whitley: did it go without saying? That aeroplane, that long lean coffin, had an affinity for the water: did anyone ever count how many went down?

So Bill Dods weighed up the pros and cons. Was it possible to alight and take off again? There was a cross-swell but the wind was not high. It was difficult, but not the kind of sea that a pilot of his experience should greatly fear. This was his last flight. In a few hours his operational tour would end and this man beside him, Gipps, would be captain from then on. It would be good to take away from the squadron the memory of a successful air-sea-rescue. It had been a tour undistinguished by notable event. So Dods framed a signal and sent it off: '*Over dinghy. May I land?*'

He flew a few more circuits. Round and round. Observing conditions down there and deciding to alight with his head into wind and the swell across his bow. Bulkheads were secured, life-jackets checked, and most of the crew climbed to the bridge to brace in ditching stations.

The reply came back from Group: '*Land at your own discretion.*'

So that was it. Dods went down into wind and across the swell as he had planned, but once there the sea looked very different. It was running high and the swell was deep. By the time he came abreast of the dinghy he had made the firm decision not to touch. Get down in there and his aircraft would be engulfed. He opened his throttles and climbed away.

'I'll try along the swell,' he said, 'and cross the wind'.

Second time down and the prospect was no more inviting.

His hand was ready on the throttles, his eye was measuring, but his instinct failed. He skidded his Sunderland onto the crest of the swell and held it there. Speed dropped off as it should have done and the aircraft remained steady and stable and apparently secure, until, with an appalling crash, a cross-swell flung it back into the air. The nose lifted and the airspeed fell and there was a lifelessness in the controls that Dods instantly read. Instantly he jammed his throttles through to the gate, for power, for lift, for every knot of airspeed he could regain. But the speed had gone and the Sunderland had to fall. Three times it fell, smothered in foam, each bounce worse than before, each time with the nose higher and the tail farther down. Bill Dods had flown his last flight and touched down for the last time. There he was, wide-eyed and helpless, defeated, clinging to the wheel as he died. With violence and sound past description, the Sunderland O plunged into an approaching swell and completely submerged.

The bows were smashed to fragments; from the cockpit forward they were torn bodily away. With the wreckage went Gipps and Dods. Farther astern, crewmen were flung about like dolls.

Back to the surface like an open-ended bottle the Sunderland surged. Tons of water streaming from it, rushing into it, flooding and swirling; awful confusion in there, where to get out, which way to go. Who is still living? Who has gone? Every man for himself for a minute or two.

Up on the mainplane they sorted themselves out. Wreckage everywhere, the Sunderland sinking in its midst. The automatic dinghy, the big one in the wing, had bloomed free and inflated as it should have done. Other dinghies were there that they dragged up from inside, but the force of impact had split them all beyond use or repair. No sign of Dods or Gipps. How could they push off until they knew where they were? Piling into the dinghy, still stunned, still shocked, still trying to count each other. How many are there? It's the skipper who's gone, and Raleigh Gipps who's gone. Everyone else by some miracle is here.

Wreckage everywhere but no Sunderland any more. Oil on the water. Fuel on the water. But something like a body away over there.

Wallace Mackie went swimming as hard as he could go, a long way in the swell heaving up and down, so far that the men in the dinghy couldn't get to him for another half-hour. Wallace Mackie found Gipps floating there, shockingly injured, barely conscious, barely alive. Mackie, the wireless operator, saved Gipps that afternoon, for half-an-hour holding his head clear and enabling him, ultimately, to survive. Gipps never flew again, but stayed alive. Dods never flew again either, and was not found.

Before dark the survivors of the Sunderland joined up with the survivors of the Whitley. They roped the dinghies together and floated on into the night. . . .

At 0040 hours next morning Gordon Singleton and crew were detailed to the search. Group hoped that two dinghies were there. The weather report was bad: 'Sea rough, fog down to fifty feet, visibility one hundred yards.'

'It's this way,' the operations officer said, 'a Wellington was over them not long ago. The pilot sighted distress flares and managed to illuminate two dinghies closely tied. That's what he saw. But the weather's grown worse. He stopped with them an hour then had to go. Finding them will be hard. But we have to try.'

Harry Winstanley was Singleton's navigator and had been for quite a while. One way and another they had flown together for a year. As navigators went Winstanley was as good as any and as pilots went Singleton had style. At 0340 they were in the air with a crew of twelve and on the way.

For an hour or two the sky was clear then a thin film of high cloud, a veil, passed between the airmen and the stars. The farther south they went the more substantial became the veil until by dawn cloud was pressing close to the sea.

Singleton went down with the cloud, lower and lower, until his world was like a mushy blanket, sea and cloud uniformly grey, and everything concealed.

Singleton had to fly almost lower than safety allowed, almost close enough to the sea for the slipstream to whip up spray, and the eyes of the pilots on the bridge and of the gunners in the turrets *strained*.

How could you see in soup of that kind? How could you see when you flew so low you were more of a ship than an aeroplane? How could you navigate without landmarks or stars or wireless aids? All that Winstanley had was his skill; no special instruments, no computers, couldn't even observe the passage of the wind on the waves. Dead reckoning was Winstanley's tool and *then* he was in the pilot's hands. Singleton had to fly on course, precisely on course, not three hundred yards this way or four hundred yards the other, straight down the middle where Winstanley put him or they might as well have stayed at home.

Three hours out and there sat the dinghies, at the edges of the murk on the starboard side. Incredible.

Singleton crossed the survivors almost at deck level, scared to reach up for height, scared to swing off to the side, scared that the moment he lost sight of them would be the moment they'd be gone. He dropped a smoke float and a marine marker to help him but you couldn't see smoke at a distance in greyness of that kind. 'I'll have to land', he said, 'now.'

Round and round Singleton flew, weighing his choices, a tight circuit keeping the dinghies in view, brushing the cloud base not a hundred feet above the sea. How could he jettison depth-charges or fuel? How could he gain height to approach for a landing in the conventional manner? None of those things could he do. The wrong way was the only way or these people in their dinghies would be not rescued today. The smoke was there; the wind direction was plain.

'Okay for landing?' he asked. 'Ditching stations? All clear?'

'All clear,' Winstanley said.

So Singleton dropped on to the greasy-looking sea, which, in fact, was an eight-foot swell, short and sharp and dangerous. Dead into wind he swung, with his nose up high and the swell running at right angles to his bow. From wave-crest to wave-crest he lightly skipped, holding that nose up, holding his aircraft up, allowing his speed to fall smoothly off until at the instant of stall he dropped her into a trough, hauled the stick into his stomach, and alighted magnificently.

After a while, when he considered his aircraft correctly fitted for taxi-ing on the open sea, he turned towards the dinghies and soon had them standing off his beam. In spite of wind and swell he brought them safely and quickly under his starboard wing and cut all engines. Dinghies and flying-boat then swung together. The survivors came in through the rear door, wet, cold, shaken, but surprisingly cheerful. Once you *know* you're 'all right', the mind can effect extraordinary physical repairs. In those fellows came, smiling, thanking everyone effusively, expressing their concern for Gipps. 'We don't really know,' they said, 'how badly he's injured internally, but it's certain you can't move him without a stretcher.'

Gipps lay on the floor of the bending dinghy, bending as the sea changed shape underneath him. He was uncomplaining. They took the top from a bunk to serve as the stretcher; too wide, unfortunately, to pass through the door flat and level, but they strapped him to it securely while the dinghy went on lurching and the aircraft went on plunging. Passing him back to the safety of the Sunderland was a rough and ready and awesome operation, with the stretcher held on edge and Gipps suspended.

On the bridge Singleton and Winstanley and the first and second pilots considered the situation—largely in silence.

There was a sense of urgency, and of growing disquiet. Bill Dods, a good flying-boat pilot, had died yesterday alighting on this piece of ocean. They heard the details. Was

74

it possible that others might die today trying to take off again?

But Gipps, below in the wardroom, was waiting.

'We've got to get him to a doctor,' said Singleton.

Outside the sea was rolling. That eight-foot swell looked interesting. The Sunderland was pitching. Out there the sea was cracking like whips against parts of the Sunderland and flooding over the floats at the wing-tips.

'We've shot ourselves with science,' said Singleton.

On board were fifteen hundred gallons of fuel and a ton of depth-charges and an operational load of ammunition and twenty-eight airmen.

'Too much dead weight, I fear,' said Singleton.

Back home on Milford Haven, where conditions were ideal, they would lift that load into the air without trying. Here it was less simple.

'We'll smash ourselves to pieces,' said Singleton. 'So where do I go from here?'

He sat with his hands to the wheel and his feet to the rudder bar keeping his aircraft into wind with extravagant movements of the controls. Those things were instinctive. But he was watching his floats with caution. Lose one and the Sunderland would turn over. And, thoughtfully, he was measuring impulse against achievement.

'Harry,' he said to Winstanley, 'what about enemy aircraft?'

'Well within their orbit. This is their country.'

That made a further interesting reflection: half-a-dozen JU 88's taking pot shots at a fat white Sunderland parked most inappropriately.

'Keep the turrets manned, Harry,' said Singleton. 'I'm wanting a sharp look-out.'

Downstairs food was being prepared and aromas were drifting incongruously. Things like stew and bread toasting. Sixteen hungry fellows to feed after a night on the ocean. To clothe also. Sixteen men to be reclad and made dry and made warmer. Singleton's crew started giving up their own clothing. Winstanley got around barefoot in his underpants.

'Harry,' said Singleton, 'if I remember correctly there's a Free French destroyer somewhere. Is it really anywhere handy?'

'We could send a signal. If you want to. But it might be intercepted.'

'If we don't send a signal how long do you think we'll be sitting here peacefully anyway?'

Winstanley coded and off it went through the aerials. But no one 'out there' acknowledged it. No one said *we hear you, we're coming*.

The cloud-base started rising. The mist started scattering. Daylight started brightening. Visibility started lengthening and suddenly they could see for miles.

Singleton sat drumming his fingers on the control column.

Ten miles away an aircraft of No 10 Squadron, heading south, picked up a radar contact. The captain altered course and began a homing run while the crew bustled hither and thither running out depth-charges and checking their weapons. But it was not a U-boat they found waiting; it was a fat white Sunderland with a signal light flashing.

'Inform Group of our condition,' said the message. 'Contact Free French destroyer and lead it to us. . . .'

The morning lengthened. The hours passed. Singleton's Sunderland pitched and drifted and tossed, its tall tail fin weathercocking in the wind. Waiting and defenceless. If it came to the worst what would your chances be in a fight?

Could you resist from the water? Could you start the engines up that you might manoeuvre a bit, that you might have electric power and hydraulic power to work your turrets and your guns and everything else you needed to convert you from a sitting duck? How long would you last? One good cannon strike would probably finish you off.

They heard the sound of Pegasus engines coming back, the Sunderland sound, and there was the aircraft of 10

Squadron sedately circling up top and there on the horizon
was a black silhouette, a ship. Topsy-turvy world, oh yes!
One Sunderland lost, one stranded, yet so close to them, a
ship? Somewhere someone, at an office desk, had not
properly stopped to think.

In came the destroyer swarming with eager Frenchmen
anxious to 'save' everybody, and stood off the bows looking
extremely warlike and chic. They lowered a whaler and
with exuberant energy made the instant mistake of rowing head-on for the Sunderland, oars flashing, backs
bending.

'*Sacrebleu,*' shrieked Singleton and abandoned his controls
to his second pilot and shot out through the open roof
screeching at the top of his voice and waving his arms and
conveying in several kinds of languages the information that
Sunderlands were sneaked upon from the rear, not bull-
rushed from the front. The Frenchmen deduced this and
Singleton went back to the tail to receive them.

A doctor came aboard and spent some time with Gipps,
and reassured them. He took Gipps away with the other
survivors, to the destroyer; all sixteen of them, though this
was not done in a single trip. On its second run-up to the
rear door of the Sunderland the whaler punched a hole
above the waterline and Singleton, though personally feeling
the pain, exercised remarkable verbal restraint. The captain
of the destroyer, perhaps to express his regret, sent across
two bottles of excellent Scotch whisky and a couple of
armourers to remove the firing pistols from the aircraft's
depth-charges. This made everyone feel safer. The Frenchmen then sent across a rope, a good long strong one, with
the suggestion that the Australians might like a tow homeward?

Whether they *liked* it or not, there was not an attractive
alternative. They could not go on drifting waiting for the
sea to become quieter—the sea was more likely to turn
rougher. Nor could they expect patrolling enemy aircraft to

go on not seeing them; that kind of luck simply could not continue. JU 88's in the Bay had never been thicker.

Singleton sent five of his crew across to the destroyer to lighten his boat further, leaving seven men aboard her. Seven could manage provided complications didn't start going crazy.

'Here's hoping,' he said to Winstanley, but there was another consideration. How would a Sunderland behave on a tow rope with that kind of sea running? It could prove to be a very dangerous experience. The five men he did not need were profoundly safer on the destroyer!

Singleton prepared for the tow by streaming a drogue under water from the keel—a drogue, one of those stout canvas bags used for mooring up and manoeuvring on difficult or confined waters. Knowing how to use your drogues was the difference between safe water-handling and disaster. This time Singleton chose to use a drogue where he had not used one before, secured to an eye in the tail end of the keel to act as a water rudder. Hall, a strong swimmer, managed to put it there from the dancing insecurity of a small rubber dinghy.

The tow-rope was then made fast to the bollard in the Sunderland's nose and Singleton signalled for the operation to begin—which it did, at once and dramatically.

Off went the Frenchmen at a vigorous ten knots, unaware that Sunderlands were delicate machines despite their deceptively rugged exteriors. Water went spraying everywhere, everything shook furiously, and seas came flooding in through the nose while all available hands frantically tried to close the turret. But the turret would not close because the tow-rope obstructed it. Water went crashing over the mainplane and into the engines, went surging into the bow compartment and pouring into the bilges. It was a most alarming development. The engineer went rushing off to try to get auxiliary power going and everybody else, with hand pumps and buckets and foul language, confessed privately to the mildest of mild panics. Up onto the top shot the wireless operator, hanging on to his Aldis lamp, flashing off signals: '*Reduce speed. Reduce speed.*' Like a cry coming from the depths of history.

'Great grief', said the French captain, or whatever it is that Frenchmen say. 'If we go any slower we'll be steaming backwards.' But cut his speed by half notwithstanding. 'Five knots,' he said gloomily, thinking of enemy aircraft and enemy torpedoes, 'we'll not be home till Christmas, if ever.'

But aboard the Sunderland this led to an improvement. They were still subjected to a shuddering and violent motion, which disturbed Singleton, but the engineer had the auxiliary motor running and the power pump working and all other hands, for the first time lately, felt they might live to talk about it afterwards. Indeed for an hour or two everything settled to a comparatively orderly and untroubled voyage, though perhaps not what they had had in mind when they left Pembroke Dock at twenty minutes to four that morning. Was theirs, they asked themselves, the only Sunderland ever to return from the Bay of Biscay at five knots behind a Frenchman? Then Hall's drogue broke.

That drogue, that sea anchor holding them straight, tore from its mountings and the Sunderland swung hard to the right, wrenching on the tow-rope, pitching and plunging; and the destroyer stopped. For which the airmen were extremely thankful.

Singleton had troubles. The sea was getting up, the wind was rising. Take-off now would be more difficult than earlier. One thing only could he do, start his starboard outer engine to counter the swing to that side and resume the tow. Something was ticking over, uncomfortably, in the back of his mind: the magnitude of the basic flaw in the idea of setting a Sunderland to catch a Sunderland, of setting a flying-boat down on the ocean. It didn't work, did it? It didn't make a tidy sum at all and became more and more unbalanced the more he thought about it.

So Singleton started up his engine, got it turning over fast enough to cancel out the swing windward and the destroyer resumed towing. But now hanging over him was the certainty of engine trouble. It was the nature of the Pegasus engine to overheat on the water, a most embarrassing defect but one that Sunderland pilots learnt to live with. You nursed those engines and when you manoeuvred on the water you got on with the job and did it quickly. Sooner or later Singleton knew he would have to throttle back and immediately he reduced power the aircraft would swing hard to starboard as it had done before.

A movement near the destroyer's stern caught his eye, a moving object.

Singleton sat a little higher.

It was a bobbing object, very close to the ship, and went sweeping into the wake, there to bob to greater purpose, most curiously, even ominously.

'I'm on course for it,' he thought. 'I can't miss it. I hope it isn't hard.'

There was a shriek from the Sunderland's bows, a clatter of boots on metal and up the companionway. '*Skipper. A mine.*'

He knew it himself at the same instant. A spherical contact mine, horns bristling. All but dead ahead and only yards distant.

Everybody died; every man blew sky high; goodbye sweet dreams; farewell, my lovely. Mined in a Sunderland on the open sea towed behind a Frenchman. No one could possibly die in that manner.

A reflex action, a nerve spasm, and Singleton was thrusting that single throttle, that starboard outer engine, wide open. Incredibly, the wing lifted its float clear of the surface and directly underneath it the mine went bobbing, down the side and into empty ocean.

Nobody said anything. What was the use of discussion? They leant against things and rubbed their faces and shook all over and waited for heartbeats to quieten.

The engineer came up from his instrument panel and tapped Singleton on the shoulder. 'Temperature's rising on the starboard outer. You'll have to nurse it.'

He nodded and crept his throttle back a little, as much as he could manage. Couldn't creep it back too far or he'd be dragged sideways through the water. The miracle of the day was that the wing-tip floats were still undamaged. The stresses they had withstood, the shocks they had weathered. All this slewing, all this thumping, all this hammering.

'Temperature's still going up, Skipper. It's getting dangerous.'

Singleton tried. At least he made the effort. Pulled the throttle back, but as soon as he touched it the aircraft veered strongly, threw its nose across its track, and was jarred severely. He *had* to open the throttle again and the engineer had to warn him: '*Switch off! Danger!*'

Singleton closed the throttle and pulled the cut-out.

The swing to starboard was violent and instantaneous and the tow-rope slackened, but the destroyer went onward and wrenched the rope taut again. The aircraft's bollard to which the rope was shackled sheared from its mounting and carried overboard.

For a moment or two they did not *comprehend* what had happened. The bollard had gone—so they would have to do without it. Then it hit them; no more bollard, no more towing: Sunderland E was loose and free and uncontrolled three hundred miles from a friendly frontier.

The destroyer hove-to and requested instructions. Instructions? Singleton could have laughed. 'I don't know,' he said to himself, 'why ask me?'

'What'll I tell them, skipper?' came the call from the man on top, the man up there with the Aldis lamp.

'I don't know,' Singleton said to himself, and looked at Winstanley, and shrugged, and looked at the sea, and held harder to the wheel. Wind and swell out there were opposed to each other by seventy degrees, a good firm wind, a good strong swell.

'I don't know,' Singleton said.

Two things only to do. Abandon his aircraft and allow the Frenchman to sink it by gunfire. Or take off.

'What'll I tell them, Skipper?'

What a choice. Take off or watch the blighters blow you up.

'Ask them to stand by,' Singleton said. 'We'll have a bash at it.'

So they ran out the depth-charges deloused by the Frenchmen and jettisoned them. They chopped away the jagged base of the bollard and closed the nose turret. They pumped the bilges dry and shut the bulkheads and hatches and took up crash positions.

'Okay,' said Singleton, 'let's get on with it.'

Which way would he go? If he headed into wind the swell would smash the aircraft to pieces. If he headed into swell the wind would be on his beam, a profound hazard. Singleton sighed, and started the engines and hardened his nerve while he brought them up to operating temperatures.

'I'll go into the swell,' he said, and opened three throttles holding the fourth at idle. With full power he would have swung at once into wind and foundered.

Three engines roaring and he could feel the boat beginning to move forward, and the explosion of sea shattering in the propellers was hair-raising. Three engines roaring, the fourth still idling, but speed was building up so slowly and visibility was nothing and the only way to steer was by instinctive prediction. Seas broke over the top of him and vibration was frightening. Seas almost swamped him. Through the seat of his pants he fought the violence, reacting with purpose and conviction to every response the aircraft made that felt sloppy or dangerous. It was an enormous, an incredible challenge; waves enveloping the bows completely, pouring in rivers over hull and windscreen; the boat plunging and rearing and thrusting and seeking always to turn windward to its destruction.

For three mad miles Singleton pressed on blindly, three throttles hard against the gate, shock and vibration continuous, his physical strength strained to the utmost, his instruments unreadable. But speed was coming, speed was growing, speed was turning into something he could handle. At sixty knots he had a responsive rudder and was opening his fourth engine, fighting off the swing through his feet, gathering real power and direction. Something changed. No longer was he battling through seas like mountains but crashing from wave-top to wave-top with startling concussion. On and on, crashing, and suddenly he was flung into the air with great violence.

The aircraft sagged beneath him, as if its interior had sunk into a hollow, as if it were at the instant of collapsing. But he caught it there and held it there and somehow sustained it by a fragile margin. A great mass of water and spray whipped from the hull and went scattering like smoke in the slipstream and the Sunderland, as if groaning, started climbing.

The intercom was silent. Nothing was said to anyone. Then, slowly, the crew began to function as if doubting that their surroundings were real or solid; a gunner moved off to midships. Winstanley bent over his table, another man kicked a hatch open and went below. Was the destroyer still out there somewhere? No one cared any longer. Winstanley gave Singleton a course for home, but everything was possessed of a peculiar feeling. Singleton remained under very great tension, but began to potter about the cockpit, adjusting the pitch, synchronizing the engines, fiddling with trimming tabs and making minor corrections. A breathless voice came into his headphones. It was Viner, the man who had gone down to the galley. 'We've been holed. I think you'd better make an inspection.'

Singleton sighed. He was not ready for that kind of

activity. 'Yes, George. I expect we have been. I'll check later.'

'This is not that sort of hole, Skipper. It's not the sort you check later.'

Singleton glanced to his second pilot and indicated that he was to take over. 'I'm coming. George.'

'Not the front way, Skipper. Come down the back into the galley.'

Singleton was assailed with a great uneasiness and went below with reluctance. Some matters were less troublesome if you didn't know everything about them.

There was a howling wind in the galley as if someone had left the hatches open, but the hatches were shut and securely fastened. Viner was waiting, with a strained and troubled expression. He took Singleton by the arm, directed him to the door of the wardroom, and steadied him.

What would you call it? Incredible? The wardroom was a heap of wreckage piled up against the bulkhead. Somehow or other the lavatory had survived but hung clanging in the slipstream. Beneath it gaped a jagged hole in the hull bottom, four feet wide, seven feet long, almost beyond acceptance.

Singleton climbed back to the bridge and looked at Winstanley blankly. 'It's huge,' he said, and went to his seat to sit awhile, thinking.

He could not alight. But can you remain airborne for ever?

Winstanley came up and shouted in his ear. 'What will you be doing?'

Singleton gestured, opening his hands emptily.

The moment he put his aircraft to water she would sink, and not gently. Not with that hole up front to swallow the ocean. She'd fracture. She'd sink violently. And every man aboard would be dead—except for miracles.

They could not bale out. There was nothing to bale out with. The squadron had decided months ago that parachutes were useless.

A landplane without wheels could land on its belly, but a flying-boat was a different conception. Every landing was a belly landing. Take away the belly and what were you left with?

'What can you do, Gordon?'

Singleton shook his head slowly.

'You mean we've had it?'

'Maybe.'

The news had travelled. All had heard. How much fuel was there? The engineer estimated that in twelve hours the tanks would be empty. Twelve hours to live was the meaning of that calculation. Unless, in the meantime, they were intercepted by the enemy. That could make it shorter.

Singleton sat there thinking.

How do you repair a hole of that magnitude? How do you rebuild a flying-boat in twelve hours without proper tools and equipment? Or do you reject the obvious and seek different solutions?

Singleton reached for his signal pad and framed a new kind of message.

'Hull caved in. Landing at Angle Aerodrome.'

He gave it to Winstanley and asked him to code it.

So Sunderland E flew back to Wales while flying-boat society politely panicked. At eight p.m. Singleton was circling the aerodrome that lay on the clifftops at the seaward end of Milford Haven, just above the waters used by the Sunderlands for night takeoff and landing.

A thousand feet beneath him turned the grass and the runways. There were the dispersal points and hangars and parked fighter aircraft. Crash-wagons and ambulances. Cars and trucks and fire-tenders and faces upturned following the course of his circuit. Everywhere else were acres of earth, hard and unyielding.

Singleton flew round sizing up his chances.

He was thinking of fire—and of a keel not designed to take the full weight of the aircraft without water to assist it. This keel was damaged and weakened. It might collapse or the bottom tear out of it. The end would be the same whichever happened.

There was a car at the end of the runway, a man in dark uniform beside it looking upwards. 461 Squadron's commanding officer. That was Douglas. Had he come to pick up the pieces?

'Are you going through with it?' asked Winstanley.

'I've got to.'

They turned out to sea and threw overboard everything movable, everything that could be picked up or torn from its mounting to reduce the weight and the stresses on the keel. Everything that might burn. Every gallon of fuel they could safely dispose of. Guns and ammunition and pyrotechnics. Pots and pans and tools. They left themselves only the soft things, the cushions and mattresses. Nothing else was valuable. Equipment that cost thousands was worthless; it did not serve the needs of survival.

Singleton flew back to land and made a dummy approach down the runway with sweat on his hands. Everything was as before; ambulances, crash-wagons, fire-tenders, up-turned faces, and *tension*. He pulled away to make a low circuit and spoke into his microphone with the calm captains found for the moments of supreme emergency. 'Captain to Navigator. Is everyone prepared for landing?'

'Navigator to Captain. Okay for landing.'

'Thank you.'

There was the runway out on his beam. All that hard ground around it. All the unknowns. He turned in towards it, into wind, and ran out full flap, lining up the Sunderland's long nose with the grass adjacent to the paved surface. The throttles were in his hand and gently he squeezed them backwards.

Down dropped Singleton, cliffs coming up to him, sea beating at the foot of them, the solid world of earth at the top of them. Thoughts frozen off from present consciousness.

Fear overcome by intense concentration. The cliffs rising up like the swell of the ocean, suddenly immediate, suddenly gone beneath him.

Flying beside the runway only feet above the surface, Douglas in his car driving flat out beside him. Flying on, nose creeping higher, speed diminishing, keel feeling for the contact, grass brushing against it.

A judder. A shuddering.

In went the step, cutting a furrow, Singleton holding on straight and level, throttling back farther, ground flashing past, lying scored behind him.

Ploughing deeper, a deeper furrow, speed decreasing rapidly and smoothly, the Sunderland turning gently and lying over, the float collapsing, the wingtip buckling unhurriedly into the grassland, engines still idling until Singleton cut them.

Was there ever a stranger Sunderland story than that one? Bill Dods began it, but another finished it.

CHAPTER SEVEN

Three's a Crowd

The great offensive against the U-boats rolled on; that was its quality, an overwhelming rolling. More aircraft were involved. More ships. More U-boats. The U-boats came out of their Biscay ports in packs and tried to batter into the Atlantic in naval tradition, running in company on the surface, relying on their combined fire-power, which was considerable, to repulse aircraft. But an odd thing happened: one of the psychological mysteries of a war full of psychological mysteries. The heavier and the more accurate and the more determined the U-boat flak became, the more accurate and the more determined the air attacks became. The Royal Navy went out into the Bay of Biscay and the German fighter wing went out into the Bay of Biscay in the kind of numerical strength it had not used before. The JU 88's hunted happily, for the odds were greatly in their favour, and there were empty beds and vacant places (I said it before), more empty beds and more vacant places than one was accustomed to living with. All this built up to an explosive battle one Friday morning that put the U-boats under the sea again and wrecked the strategy of defensive formation for the duration of the war.

The 'picture' was vast. It always was. It usually reached to the ends of the earth. You didn't personally see that far; simply a daub on a part of the board; but the experts assured you, probably rightly, that if you created an effective disturbance in one place the reverberations were felt everywhere. Someone once told me that if you stamped a foot you shook the planet.

This particular action began at 45 degrees 42 minutes North, 11 degrees West, and ended not a great distance from there, but embraced air and sea for hundreds of miles around. Its immediate strategic effects reached as far west as the Caribbean. Its immediate human effects were more complex and more difficult to decide. Human effects are beyond calculation. Many young lives ended that day and there were great celebrations.

At 0945, Greenwich Mean Time, Liberator O of 53 Squadron, R.A.F., was flying south down 11 degrees West. About sixty miles astern of him the Second Escort Group of the Royal Navy, five ships, also steamed in that direction. Elsewhere, beyond the invisible depths of the compass points, the usual odd assortment of aircraft flew their separate and lonely but alert patrols. 0945 hours—that was the moment Liberator O sighted three U-boats tra elling in a V at close to maximum surface speed on a south-westerly heading, a heavily armed formation of supply ships laden with fuel and provisions (and mail from home) and munitions for the fighting 500 tonners waiting in mid-Atlantic. What a sight it was to come upon.

Could he attack? Could one Liberator plausibly go plunging into action? Not only did he see them, they saw back again, and manoeuvred to confront him with the full face of their armament. Discretion, perhaps, was a more constructive contribution to victory than headstrong bravery. So up went the Liberator to higher altitudes sending off its sighting report and transmitting the homing signals for other aircraft to tune in to. Out of range of the U-boats guns, like a beacon on a high mountain.

First in was Sunderland R of 228 Squadron, R.A.F., a unit sharing Pembroke Dock with the Australians. The captain of R circled the perimeter but considered that only a lunatic would attempt to attack unaided. Through binoculars he watched the German gun barrels following him.

Another aircraft came in low and fast from an easterly direction, a strange sight in those days, a single Junkers 88, unaccompanied. Usually they came in sections or flights or squadrons. At 11 degrees West he must have been as far from land as he could safely venture. Like a terrier he went for the Sunderland at double its airspeed, sending it scattering, sending it climbing for cloud cover, forcing its captain to jettison his depth-charges. You couldn't fight a combat with a bellyful of high explosive and hope to get out of it. Down went the depth-charges tumbling over and over— which was all that mattered that morning. The 88 broke off the attack (could the laughter be heard?) and let the Sunderland go.

Up on top the Liberator circled, still beaming its signals for everyone to hear, friend and foe. In they were coming, still unseen, from everywhere around, homing on those signals, direction-finding aerials tuned. The 88 went away. A Catalina arrived. Sunderland R came down again from the cloud. Another Liberator flew in, with Americans at the controls. The Catalina headed up north to find the Royal Navy ships and bring them down. Two R.A.F. Halifaxes appeared. Lots of aircraft going round and round, one after the other, trying to pluck up the courage to get in there and try.

The U-boats on the surface were travelling now at maximum speed, about twenty knots (Under water, four knots was as much as they could do.) Still in their V formation, making zig-zags and tight S-turns, still heading for the Atlantic, still presenting the full concentration of fire-power to each aircraft that looked as though it might be about to batter through. Flak stood up like a fence, like an explosive wall: there was just too much of it. You didn't achieve anything by throwing your life or your aircraft away. There had to be a hope or you were simply a fool. If your life had

to be given, there had to be an exchange. You were not
flying a fighter aircraft, after all. You were not at the
controls of a Spitfire. You had a slow and lumbering and
large machine, and you had a crew.

Admiral Doenitz, with his mass formation on the surface,
must have been at the brink of a major breakthrough. They
must have been feeling pretty good down there. 'We've
stopped the so-and-so's,' they must have been saying. 'We've
licked the aeroplane and about time, too.'

A Sunderland of 461 Squadron turned home from a long
and uneventful patrol near Spain; twelve men on board,
captained by Dudley Marrows, a pilot of some experience
and competence. He had never attacked a U-boat, had
never been involved in a death-or-glory combat; at least,
not until that day; lots of hard work over hundreds and
hundreds of arduous flying hours, but the action was always
happening when he wasn't around.

That day he had seen a few fishing vessels of assorted
kinds, but not the 88's that so often turned up when fishing
vessels were found. Non-combatant fishing vessels and highly
combatant Junkers 88's had a touching affinity. Suspiciously,
perhaps? Were they *really* fishing? Who could say? The
doubt was always there and you had to behave, you were
not allowed to open fire. But often you wondered as you
flew by and they waved.

Marrows and his men heard the sighting report from
Liberator O, but scarcely blinked an eye. It would not be
for them. After all, it was two hundred miles away; another
ocean, another world. No U-boat in history had waited for
a heavy-footed Sunderland to cover two hundred miles.

'Thanks,' said Marrows, to the report from his wireless
operator. 'That's interesting, I'm sure.' But didn't increase
airspeed or alter course or think hopefully of it at the time.

In a minute or two the wireless operator was on the
intercom again. 'W/T to Captain, there's a message for us here.'

'Let's have it please.'

'We've been directed to 45.42 North, 11.00 West. That's the U-boat pack, skipper. That's where it is.'

'*Directed* there?' said Marrows, and glanced at Leigh in the first pilot's seat. 'All right. I suppose we'd better go. If you'll give me a course, Navigator, please?'

Rolland gave Marrows the heading to fly but lodged a warning with it as well. 'Keep your hands off the throttles, Captain. Don't waste fuel with extra speed. If you have to make an attack you'll be needing every gallon in your tanks to get us home. We've had a heavy day.'

'I'll watch it,' said Marrows, but in an uncommitted way. Fuel needed for attacking U-boats? U-boats on the surface? Two hundred miles farther along the road home? He was sure there would not be a battle for this aircraft or its crew today, but the God of War was sitting on a cloud nearby, sharpening up his sword, laughing at these mortals who couldn't read the signs.

U-461 was the submarine in formation on the starboard side. U/461 was the Sunderland Marrows was flying home. If that was not the set-up for a deadly consummation on a summer's day, nothing ever had been since man became aware that fate did not plant its seeds to be ignored.

But at the scene of the encounter the other principals were reluctant to engage; the aircraft still circled outside the range of fire, the Second Escort Group had not arrived, the U-boats still travelled in formation towards the western sky; a curious kind of stalemate it was for a while as if no one wished to cast the first decisive stone. Halifax B turned out to be the man.

In he went, ponderously, in a high state of nerves, sixteen hundred feet above the sea. His weapon was new, the six-hundred pound anti-submarine bomb, that one did not aim in a moment of glory from the top of the trees. In he tracked beneath the clouds, with a bomb-aimer up front consulting his instruments and calling the course changes to bring him in true. For the captain it was easy theoretically: 'Fly it straight, boy. Track steady. Dodge the flak. Survive.' None of this Sunderland stuff where the captain did everything short of instructing the enemy whether to shoot back or dive.

So in he swung as the U-boats turned to show him the muzzles of their guns. Every gun on every U-boat simultaneously shooting at him. A bursting sky he lumbered through, brave and steady and straight, a flak target as perfect as flak could have, to deliver a weapon (that A/S bomb) designed by fools, or vested interests, or very old men who hated youth. The U-boats hit him but he did not hit them: three bombs he dropped and the nearest missed by seventy yards. On flew the Halifax captain, weaving out of the flak, avoiding destruction by some remarkable turn of luck. On he flew and away. What was the use now of turning back? 'Home,' he said to his navigator. 'Let's go. Give me a course.'

The second Halifax climbed to make height for an attack. Up he went, weighing the fors and the againsts. Up he went to three thousand feet considering that at higher levels flak danger might be reduced. The captain of this aircraft was angry and Dutch. For two hours he had circled the U-boats while they had rushed into the west, waiting for the sun to come out, for the clouds to drift clear, for his stage to be precisely set. There the sun blazed, and out of the middle of it came Dutch, undulating through the flak lines, keeping the sun on his tail where it dazzled the gunners who were trying to blow him to bits. They threw shells all around him, but he found his way through without a scratch. (God was on his side; had to be; no other explanation; they should have been able to hit him with bricks.) Three six-hundred pound bombs dropped. . . .

Marrows was coming, cruising quietly north.

Must have been getting close. Watching the fuel position now with curious concern. Where had it all gone? Had he sprung a leak? 'An awful lot of petrol we've used,' he kept saying to himself. 'Not that it'll matter. We'll not be needing extra. U-boats on the surface? No such luck.'

'First Pilot here, Captain,' Leigh said, talking into his mike. 'Out there on the starboard. Three destroyers, I think. Fifteen miles.'

Marrows sat up straight and peered out. Beautiful sunlight and the kind of blueness you saw more often farther south. 'Yes,' he said, 'I see them. Get the binoculars on them, Jimmy. Destroyers aren't much use to us.'

Leigh brought the glasses into focus and Marrows turned until the destroyers were dead ahead. Twelve miles now— Sunderland aircrew measured distance with uncommon accuracy by educated guess. 'First Pilot to Captain. They're not destroyers, they're U-boats, by gosh. I see shell-splashes and aircraft and from here what looks like an attack.'

That took some getting used to. U-boats on the surface, *still* on the surface, and under attack! Marrows almost had to think about it, almost had to question it, before he thrust the nose down and put the mixture into rich. What was petrol now except the stuff of flight? If you used it, you used it. So what. He switched on the intercom. 'Captain to all positions. We're going to be in it. I think. Test your weapons. Run the bombs out. Get the sighting report off to Base. Install the galley guns and stand by them. I don't want anyone feeling he's left out.'

Then Marrows said to himself: 'They've waited. They've stayed put. Two hours of sitting on the surface? What sort of game is that?'

Five miles ahead of him now, there they were, throwing up a screen of flak so heavy the shadowing aircraft were forced to circle miles out. It came as a surprise: not a man aboard had imagined U-boat anti-aircraft fire to be as formidable as that. In the far north a Halifax had apparently disengaged and was flying off. Closer, a second Halifax appeared to be tracking across the enemy formation at the incredible altitude of three thousand feet. What was the idiot doing up there? Was he *hoping* for an early death? Shell-bursts in the air like a measles rash.

Three bombs spilled from the Halifax. THREE BOMBS (would you believe it?) went falling through flak and Marrows blinked. Was it an aberration? Was it some new, demented technique? Not a Sunderland captain alive could have viewed it with less than shock. Marrows was *astonished* when the bombs fell close enough to produce some kind of result. The U-boat on the left swung hard to starboard and for a time went into a circular course pouring smoke from damage aft.

'Cripes,' said Leigh.

Sunderland U/461 reached flak range and joined the shadowing circuit at a thousand feet. A foot higher was unthinkable. Even a thousand feet was rarefied-level stuff. Boat crews started feeling giddy if they couldn't count the fish. (True. The higher you went the more insecure you felt, a paradox, and contrary to the basic common-sense facts of flight.)

'Control to Captain,' Rolland said. 'Everything is ready for an attack.'

'Thank you.' (As if the furniture had been re-arranged for a light-hearted party in the Mess.)

'We'll take the fellow on the left,' Marrows said. 'A U-boat damaged is not a U-boat sunk and he might be easier to get. Let's see if we can give him a fright.'

But that damaged U-boat, like a wounded animal, was effective in defence, more so than the others perhaps, even though down by the stern and making black smoke.

Marrows dived into the barrage and like troops on parade, the three U-boats turned beam on. Up came the lot, every barrel as one. It was the Sunderland, not the U-boats, that had the fright.

'Too hot,' Marrows said, and pulled out, weaving and undulating in broad sweeps of flight that the enemy might not predict his position and score hits.

'W/T to Captain. There's an American Liberator wanting to speak with us.'

'Switch him through.'

The American said, 'This stuff's too thick for one aircraft. We've got to divide it with simultaneous attacks. Will you come with me?'

To Marrows that sounded like the right approach. 'Yes,' he said.

'Let's finish off this guy on the port.'

'Let's,' Marrows said.

Four hundred yards apart the two aircraft turned in and went undulating down towards the sea, but again the U-boats swung beam on and slammed up a box barrage that was much too thick. Both aircraft climbed steeply out and throttled back.

'It's tough,' the American said.

Marrows flew on round the circuit, out of flak range, trying to think through his problem. It was not acceptable that he should admit defeat or afterwards he would reproach himself. ('What did you do in the war, Daddy?' 'Looked after my aircraft, son. Didn't even scratch the paint.')

In the two and a quarter hours since the attack had begun no one had been able to penetrate at low level. Admiral Doenitz and his superbly disciplined crews had all but beaten the aircraft. Had, at long last, the aeroplane come to its crisis point?

Four were left. The English Liberator—the fellow who had started it off; the American Liberator; the Australian Sunderland; and the Dutch Halifax still with a couple of bombs on the racks. Four aircraft, and the same conclusion had been reached by each; attack at deck-level through that defence would almost certainly end in death, unless it were possible to approach the U-boats head-on and remain head-on by out-turning them. But what aircraft could achieve that kind of manoeuvre outside the fantasies of fiction? It would end as before, with all U-boats beam on and all guns head-on. Deck-level suicide. It might be hoped that even the Brass Hats in London did not expect that.

It was the Englishman who went next, Liberator O/53, R.A.F. For him it was harder than for the rest. He had had an age to think. Two and a half hours to circle the scene and watch. But his signalling duty was finished up top. There were no more aircraft to home in; every aircraft in range had already arrived or left. Such a long time he had had to think and the longer a man thought the harder it got. The longer the deliberation the more complicated the plot. But he went. In cold blood, heroically, he went. The things that young men do. These terrible events.

Down he dived, straight and true, almost onto the surface of the sea and with smooth precision the U-boats again swung beam on, as the Englishman had expected they would, and in front of him and around him they filled the air with the elements of death. On he went into the midst of them, replying with every gun his crew could aim back, shells and shrapnel tearing his aircraft to tatters. Bits, outside the pilot's window, ripping off.

In the Sunderland's intercom Marrows' voice came harshly, 'Give me the lot, Jimmy. We're going after him.'

Pitch fully fine. Mixture fully rich. Throttles wide open. Everything flat out, howling and shaking, the exciting scream of power, its thunder and its vibration; the sounds that young men live and die by. Over swung the Sunderland in Marrows' hands, steeply down with all the thrust its engines had, a mile behind.

The Englishman flew on, somehow surviving, somehow controlling his aircraft with pieces breaking off, repeatedly hit, sea and air around him a mass of smoke and tracer fire and shell-splashed spray, turning in towards the submarine with Marrows' number on it, U-461. If he had picked another he might have won his day. The Englishman battered on and stayed in the air and dropped his depth-charges but knew they had fallen uselessly wide. Suddenly his aircraft was through its Armageddon and out into the open air on the other side, not a shell-burst to be seen, not a tracer in view. Like Alice through the looking-glass into wonderland. At a thousand yards every gun switched as one to Dudley Marrows at point-blank range.

Up came the flak in ranks, in blocks of fire and smoke (was there a piece with *your* name on it?), but Marrows held his speed and dive and struggled like a giant to bring the boat into line. He was too far out, too far off side, and made a beautiful target for shooting down, but his own gunners couldn't get the aim and on the starboard a shell went through his mainplane; an enormous physical effort, an enormous emotional effort, an enormous strain, but somehow he got that U-boat into line, *magnificently*. In he flew, perfectly straight, down on the surface, feet only between keel and sea, head-on to the enemy fire, so low and so skilfully placed that not a gun on the other U-boats could be brought to bear. Pearce, down beneath Marrows' feet in the Sunderland's nose, found line and range and with one small Vickers .303 swept the enemy gunners overboard, as if each man had been personally lifted up and thrown; in an instant their lives gone. In an instant more, in a moment of onward-rushing alarm, the U-boat was there, so close to Marrows he almost hit the conning-tower, so low there were inches only in between. Seven depth-charges plummeted across the forward deck and Marrows burst into the zones of fire of the other submarines, but at once the American swung in from the far side. Up went Marrows, violently weaving through the flak, flying with all his great strength, and the tail gunner, astonished beyond belief, witnessed an immense eruption of foam and debris thundering up from the surface of the sea. Within it the long lean U-boat snapped like a stick.

Fire switched, suddenly off Marrows, suddenly onto the American, suddenly into his face, but he went through it headlong, aiming for the other side boat. A shell burst in his bomb-bay, that awful impact underneath, should have blasted him to bits, but on he went and in, his gunners sweeping all life from the submarine's decks, but his depth-charges failed to fall from the racks. Everything in the bomb-bay was wrecked.

Marrows reached the sweeping apex of his climb and turned to attack again. Flak puffs and tracer lines started weaving his way, but the two surviving U-boats were drawing out of range. He went down towards the brilliant orange pool of debris and oil and scum that had been U-461 as the Dutchman came in at two thousand feet making his second run. U-462 again, for the Dutchman, the boat on the other wing. Flak again, almost as much as before. All the way he had to fight his way in and his bombs fell close enough to damage it aft again. Almost at once its decks appeared to be awash and crewmen started swarming up from its interior, inflating dinghies and abandoning ship.

Marrows ran in on the remains of U-461. About thirty men were in view, trying to reach wreckage that might remain afloat, trying to stay alive though chances now were remote. How many were dead? How many maimed? How many at this moment were trapped in air pockets in one broken half or the other as the bits sank far underneath? Over went the Sunderland crew, low and fast, no bullets fired, no weapons used, pushing their main dinghy-pack out through the back, giving the enemy the dinghy they might yet need themselves. (My God, raged the Brass Hats, this has got to stop, and two days later forbade aircrews to drop life-saving equipment after U-boat attacks. Not that the prohibition significantly altered the facts.)

But Marrows was pulling away, going on and up, still with a depth-charge left, still with a target to drop it on, that centre U-boat, U-504, still on the surface at maximum surface-speed, heading west. Marrows went after it, cutting off the miles, but ran into a mass of flak that startled him almost out of himself; everywhere, spread across the sea and across the enemy and around about like a picket fence.

'Midships to Captain.' A cry it was. 'Starboard beam. Five ships. They're firing.'

Were they ever!

Marrows broke off his run with fierce undulations. The ships of the Second Escort Group were plunging in from the north, down from the north they had come, the officer in command signalling *General Chase* for one of the rare occasions since the time of Nelson, five ships abreast at full speed, grey steel, white wakes, blue sky, green sea. So they had come and so they arrived, to bombard the sea where the U-boat was; not the sort of opposition the Germans could dismiss with anti-aircraft weapons and a four-inch gun. They crash-dived. How sad. In went the aircraft again and dropped marine markers over the swirl, tongues of smoke in the sea like lilies. White lilies. Down underneath, undamaged, the U-boat and its men. Should the commander of U-504 have read the signs and stayed on the surface and played his luck? One can be wise, looking back. We were not often wise, not any of us then. Even now how simple is the wisest of men.

An uneasy calm came over that sea. Out of the sea all life came, they tell us. Dozens of tiny one-man dinghies, there they were, and brilliant stains and oil patches and rubbish and bodies and smoke lilies and five frigates so lovely, so sleek, so indifferent to human life.

The American set course for his Base, the Dutchman set course for his Base, and Marrows flew across to report. . . . Two U-boats sunk, Marrows said; there are numbers of survivors, the position of the third is fixed with marine markers. . . . Then a voice spoke to Marrows; his Flight Engineer: 'You've used your fuel, Captain. There's not enough left to get us back.'

The Englishman in Liberator O failed to get home also. No hope of reaching England, so went the other way. Across two hundred miles of ocean his aircraft held together, long enough to reach Portugal, long enough to crash-land.

Kite and *Woodpecker* and *Wild Goose*, three pretty little ships, at once went a-hunting, went a-plastering with asdic and depth-charges and crushing efficiency. Oil came up first, in patches, then welled up in great volume, bubbles of oil bursting. Wood came up and wreckage and clothing and every man aboard U-504 perished.

Admiral Doenitz got the message. So did a few families and other interested persons. No more fighting it out in packs on the surface. The aeroplane's moment of crisis was its moment of victory. Seventy men the ships then picked up from the ocean, but Marrows did not wait around to see it. 'Try for the Scillies,' said Rolland, 'that's the nearest land that's friendly.' The Scillies; at the toe of England, islands in the Atlantic. (We used to touch down there sometimes to practise surreptitiously alighting on the ocean—with land close enough to swim to!)

'Will we make it?' Marrows said.

But the rest of the crew gave little thought to it. Excitement and reaction and varying degrees of bewilderment dominated them. Fuel? What was that? They'd get home. They'd make it. Navigators and engineers and pilots were always worrying over minor technicalities. After all, the greatest single victory of the war against U-boats in the Bay of Biscay was not won every day of the week. And there were other matters of significant importance—trying to accept the incredibilities. Their huge aircraft, safely through that exploding wall of death; how had it happened? Not a man hurt, not a scratch, not a blister; how had *that* happened? And in the other aircraft, in all of them, even in aircraft torn and tattered, not a life lost, not an injury. Looking back: how extraordinary.

There were times when one felt one had to accept the obvious; the gods of war had favourites, though they were likely to withdraw their graces without notice.

'Nose to Control. U-boat on the starboard bow.'

Marrows, preoccupied by his thoughts—getting over the shock of everything, trying to adjust to the probability of a mid-ocean ditching—snapped back to awareness. That was Watson's voice, Paddy's voice, that southern Irishman with the devil's own sense of humour. It was not always advisable to take Paddy at face value; this was just the sort of lark he would get up to; and there was laughter on the intercom, fellows here and there switching on and off again. Intercom discipline had relaxed a little; Marrows had not had the heart to insist upon it.

But Paddy Watson wasn't laughing.

'Nose here. Will you listen to me! I tell you there is a U-boat! Forty degrees starboard. One and a half miles!'

Marrows squinted at Leigh and switched on his microphone. A joke was a joke, but this was ridiculous. 'Now look here, Paddy,' Marrows said firmly, 'you're seeing spots, my boy. . . .

'Suffering cats. . . .' said Marrows.

'*It is a U-boat.*'

A stunned silence.

'I'm going straight in,' bawled Marrows. 'Get the bomb out! Slap in the galley guns! Grab the camera!'

He dropped from two thousand feet in a straight dive without evasive action, without thought for anything but fuel and sudden attack and swift getaway. At a range of a thousand yards, seconds elapsed only, still steeply diving, he was ready for action and had caught the U-boat off guard— or perhaps in the actual moments of surfacing. Watson had already opened fire and was spraying the decks to keep the submariners dodging and everybody else aboard the Sunderland was still blinking and Marrows was measuring height against distance and the U-boat's course against his own and credibility against incredibility. Up came the U-boat's flak, suddenly, and a multiple stream of tracers and explosive shells all but engulfed him. There was a sense of impact, of being hit, of an explosion in the wing root.

Still diving, everything beautifully measured, still head-long into the flak, smoke pouring from the Sunderland and no one knowing it, Marrows with a thumb on the bomb button, but beginning to exert the force that would lift the nose of the Sunderland across the conning-tower of the enemy. Beginning to increase that force, beginning to *strain* on the wheel, beginning to *wrench* at it, because nothing was responding. The Sunderland still was diving and would not come out of it. *Controls jammed.* The ultimate horror of a pilot's nightmare.

'Jimmy!' Marrows bellowed. 'Help me!'

Leigh grasped the dual controls and both men fought together, but sea and flak and U-boat rushed still closer through seconds as long as hours, two hundred knots on the air-speed indicator, everything point-blank, everything instantaneous, thumb hard against the bomb button, and Marrows' feet and Leigh's feet braced against the instrument panel, straining, heaving, supremely trying. The U-boat filling the world, its crewmen and gunners in horror hurling themselves flat, a shattering instant of indecision between life and death, literal inches between keel and U-boat deck, and the Sunderland was squashing into even flight at sea-level, spinning spume behind it, and smoke.

'Galley here. We're on fire in the bomb room.'

'Tail here. No depth-charge, Captain. It didn't drop.'

But Marrows and Leigh, profusely streaming sweat, still fought on at sea-level, somehow holding the boat up, some-how dragging it a few feet higher though it wanted most earnestly to dive into the ocean, frantically winding on the trim to bring the nose up, and their muscles aching and their limbs shaking and Marrows grunting, 'I don't know how long we'll be holding this.' And Pearce was tumbling down the companionway from the engineer's panel to the galley grabbing fire-extinguishers as he went.

Where was the U-boat? Astern somewhere, recovering

from a violent fright, zig-zagging at every knot it could produce, while Marrows and Leigh struggled to gain more height. Then the U-boat's decks were deserted and its hatches shut and it crash-dived out of sight—which released everyone from a dangerous and embarrassing situation.

'Engineer to Captain. The fire was in the traverse motor. I've put it out. And your bomb-gear's half shot away. That's why your depth-charge didn't drop.'

Marrows and Leigh struggled on and up, with course set for the Scillies again, but with the chance of arrival frailer than ever. By sheer brute strength they dragged the aircraft up to a thousand feet, but if they *did* reach the Scillies how would they get down safely in one piece? How could you alight in an aircraft like this? How could you lift its nose high enough to make a safe approach? It was beyond the limits of human strength. Something would have to snap if you went on applying pressure as desperately as this. Something mechanical or something human, and the outcome was instant destruction no matter which.

'Captain to Engineer. The controls are damaged, badly I think, but I'm hanged if I can work it out. Shell damage would have severed them. How could it make them stick? Something must be jammed. Something's shifted. Have a look.'

Off went Pearce, all along the cables, all along the catwalk, fore to aft and back. 'Engineer to Captain. No damage that I can see. Nothing stuck in them. Nothing shot up.'

Marrows glanced at Leigh, Leigh beside him, braced, still with hands to the wheel, his brow knotted with strain and glistening with sweat. It looked bad, but that was how it went. Suddenly, unaccountably, your luck would run out. But why, if in the affected area you were not hit? An uneasy sensation, half elation, half guilt, sent Marrows 'eyes sharply to his left. The automatic pilot. There it was. Set!

The relief. . . .

In the rush of the attack, left arm thrown out to fuse the

depth-charge, had his sleeve fouled the lever and slipped it into *locked*? Locked going down? Locked with the aircraft in a diving attitude? Did it matter now how it had happened or with what? He slipped the lever out (so lightly to finger touch) and the wheel came loose and there they sat, the two pilots, trembling back to calmness, marvelling at the chatter on the intercom, all those other fellows, so carefree and victory-flushed, not for a moment worrying about death-dives or petroleum products.

Marrows worked everything out again, setting mixture and throttles and pitch and airspeed in delicate balance one with the other to stretch range to the utmost. It was text-book flying—and had to be. He prayed for no enemy aircraft and no enemy ships and no headwinds and for a quiet, quiet alighting in the Scillies.

He made it. (The crew had never doubted that he would.) Down he thumped in the channel outside the village of St Mary's with enough petrol left to shine a small kitchen sink.

Six weeks later Dudley Marrows and crew—many of them on the last trip they were required to make to complete their operational tours—failed to return from patrol. Ten miles from the scene of their successful assault on submarine U-461 they were attacked by six Junkers 88's and shot down, their aircraft on fire, all turrets dead, three engines silent, a shambles from stem to stern. For one hour they had fought with great spirit while Marrows flew his crippled aircraft with brutal and unrelenting strength, yet landed it almost in bits on a twelve foot swell with the lightness of a bird. Marrows didn't lose a man.

Next morning they were rescued by H.M.S. *Woodpecker*, flagship of the Second Escort Group, the ship that had taken up from the sea the German survivors of U-461. Fate played a heavy hand with Dudley Marrows, but let him off the hook.

CHAPTER EIGHT

On Patrol

When you started your operational tour it was very much an emotional experience. People vary; perhaps some (many for all I know) felt the pressures less, but one's *spirit* was kept out of view, not shared, and not talked about. Not at any time did I discuss the terrors I lived with, not even with the most special girl. The likelihood of *that* was even more remote. Chivalry and bravado were not dead then. The division of the sexes was clear. Men did not give way or weep. If a boy fell short of public expectation he was a coward and often it was the girl who told him, or her mother told him, or a white feather came in the post. No psychological sugaring of the pill, no delicate shade of meaning.

The boy–girl relationship was a game of set procedures and rules. Rarely was it honest in present-day terms of honesty. Generally it was a pose, a posturing, not that poses and posturing have gone out of fashion, but the poses of that time would be loudly off-key if young people assumed them now.

When a boy put on that uniform, when he identified himself as aircrew with white flash or badge or wing, he grew a few inches and squared his shoulders and strutted just a little. The girl on his arm strutted a little too. His clean-cut character (almost a cliché), his grooming, his bearing, his high standards of personal conduct lifted him—and her—above the crowd. Through him she was aircrew too. Through him she fought too. His uniform was her status symbol. Together, their bravery was proclaimed for all to see.

The boy still in civilian clothes had a rough time. Even if she had been his girl for years she started showing reluctance or impatience or indifference when he came around. One is not making moral judgements—that would be too easy now and totally unfair—but boy and girl were products of their time, tailored by circumstances or Nature or need or the propaganda of centuries, tailored to the year and the day.

How often a girl following the crowd or the creed, by conforming to the ethos of her Age, by a word or a glance has driven the boy she loved to his death, then spent the rest of her life mourning him.

It was not *done* for a well-bred girl to try to save her love no matter what her private anguish had to be; nor was it *done* for a well-bred boy to choose love or life before war. To choose *aircrew*, to pass the stringent physical tests, to meet the demanding requirements of intelligence and aptitude, to volunteer for the high risk of death by violence and fire was to receive the community's seal of approval upon you and your family and your girl. What went on privately in your mind or in the minds of your family or in the heart of your girl it was not proper to discuss or reveal. Nobody really knew what anybody else felt. Nobody really understood the other's point of view. So history wrote itself and everyone allowed it to happen.

The aircrew boy assumed a mask of bravery and dash and calm. As aircrew it was expected of him. One could say he was popularly believed to be fearless. There was much confusion between bravery and fearlessness; too many people regarded the two qualities as the same. The man fortunate enough or insensitive enough to be fearless had no need for bravery; the ordinary young fellow with a healthy sense of fear lived a life of much greater intensity, much greater strain. It was never made clear to him that bravery was the overcoming of fear. Privately, *very privately*, he probably regarded himself as a coward and sooner or later lay awake at night *stunned* by the realization of what he had done, of the job he had given himself, of the moment he had come to, numbed by the anticipation of trying to deal with it, of trying to cope with it. When it came to the pinch would he break?

Some did break and were sent away, quietly, from squadron or operational training unit bearing the brand, L.M.F., on personal documents. *Lack of moral fibre.* Confidential. Very. But it managed to get around! People heard.

The first operational flight was the hurdle. It stood a mile high before you. What life would be like beyond the hurdle you couldn't say, you could not imagine, but there was the hope it would be less overwhelming. Fellows who had done twenty trips or thirty trips, fellows who had five hundred operational hours, you regarded with awe, with wonderment. What wisdom and maturity and greatness were theirs. They, in turn, ached for their future—the unattainable, the infinite. Eight hundred operational hours. Then the death sentence would expire and they would be set free. 'Well done good and faithful servant: enter thou into the joy of thy Lord.'

For a mile, or was it two?, I sat in a motor vehicle with Dudley Marrows, from the railway station to the guard house or something of the kind. Years haze the memory of where; nothing hazes the memory of the whisper in my ear. 'That's Flight Lieutenant Marrows, D.S.O., D.F.C.'

Greatness like that? Was it given to living men? My spirit sank, and sank, and almost ceased to be.

It was said there were two flights when danger was extreme—the first and the last. There was little to choose between them. There came a day when operational tours were less rigid, when hours flown or trips made did not have to meet predetermined totals. This was a humane breath and many survived who might have perished. A hand would fall upon your shoulder and the Commanding Officer would say, 'Son, I think you've had enough. You've finished your tour. Pack your bags.' And you were spared the last flight when every nerve was tautened and the world turned upside down. You were spared because your last flight was behind you, gone, before you were told. None of this fitted the public image of the intrepid young pilot going his way with dash and verve, but it was nearer the real image for most I fear, though many may not admit it, even now. By the time you were 'finished', you were whacked, you were through.

But you had to start before any of that began.

I went to the squadron when losses had been heavy; losses were still going on; it was 'one of those times'. Got on well with the fellow in the next bunk. Knew him for a week. Took me down town and introduced me to the girls at the Y.W.C.A. Woke up one morning and he was gone. Dead. Shot down. He was too young to die. So was I.

You tossed at nights and you turned. No breathing from the next bed. Did he die by bullet or fire or impact or did he drown? I'd drown. It was even in my records. Non-swimmer. So they posted me to Coastal Command.

'You'll have to learn to swim,' they said at the Personnel Reception Centre before they put me on the train for Wales, 'or you'll drown. No need to wait to get shot at, lad. Just fall off the pier or slip from the mainplane or miss your footing when you're jumping aboard. And drown.'

'Can't swim, sir. I sink. I go straight down.'

'Nonsense,' they said. 'Everyone can swim; even you, if you try.'

So they chucked me in the Brighton public baths. Glop. 'Swim, lad,' they cried, 'if you don't we'll leave you to drown.'

So I sank. So I went straight down and they fished me out with a boat hook every time. 'Can't post you to Coastal Command. That's mad.' But I went just the same.

You waited, numbed, for the first operational flight to come around. Joined your crew. Learnt the rudiments of your new trade. Second pilot. *Third pilot*, if one wished to split hairs. They trained you on ops at that time; weren't enough trained *third pilots* to meet demands. You were the office boy, the general hand, the cleaner, the messenger, the doormat. The sorcerer's apprentice.

God, you felt awful. Any day now you'd die. Yet you felt proud. You'd sit in the captain's seat on the Sunderland's bridge (when no one else was around) and make-believe. But that aircraft was so huge in its day, so daunting for the novice, and outside was the lapping sea. If you were like me you had never sailed a boat in your life, never set a sail, couldn't pick a current from a tide or a channel from a sand-bar, yet one stormy night you were suddenly tossed aboard to *look after* the Sunderland, to ride out the gale, with a fitter to start the engines if required and a couple of luckless air gunners to watch the buoy.

Meanwhile, you prayed.

Just to make certain that God was kindly disposed, you slipped a stout New Testament in the left breast-pocket of your battledress and gave it extra body with a steel mirror. Not until years later did I hear the rumour that the heart was nearer the centre than the side. As for the Testament I have it still, acquired in America, with a standard printed message inside from President Roosevelt about being a good boy. I never flew an operational patrol without it. Never. In the other pocket of the battledress, on the right—there was a lung in there, after all—you squeezed a heavy metal case packed with concession-priced cigarettes. (That was something else I heard later; the need to knock the smoking habit; only took twenty years.) And you continued to pray. I was glad of ONE ear into which I could unload my fear and panic and distress. Young men of my upbringing did not require psychiatrists in those days. One's faith was simple, one's trust was intact. Was that why we did not confide, totally, in each other?

Each night at dinner the Operations List was pinned to

the board. Each night you checked it, waiting for the call. Each night you read it, uncertain whether you wanted to face it now or never at all. Then it came and with it the appalling sense of *now*. There was your captain's name. There was the time of take-off: 0100 hours. That was your death sentence. There it was on the wall.

Seven o'clock. Everyone else heading off into the evening for a riotous time. But you were in bed, listening to a thudding noise that would not permit you to sleep. Your heart, thudding everywhere. Was it keeping the rest of the crew awake?

It was a dormitory. I remember it now. A hospital ward it had been once, until bombs wrecked it back in 40/41. So they turned it into a place for aircrew to sleep, patched it up, concreted the floors, painted out the window-panes, and in we went. Second coldest place I ever lived in, I think.

Three hours I lay there until ten o'clock, sometimes so short of air I had to open my mouth and gulp for breath.

'Are you awake?' someone asked.

So you sat up and started struggling into your flying kit, arranged in painfully precise order all over the empty bed standing next. Jack's bed, not a week empty; Jack, not a week dead.

A shockingly cold night. Hit you outside like a premeditated act. So dark out there, so unsympathetic; a long way to grope clopping in great boots to the aircrew mess. Bacon and eggs, they gave you. Never anything else. Pre-flight rations. Extra special stuff. Not so many eggs around in those days, not much bacon. Amazing where the appetite came from. Sometimes, if you were lucky, you could back up for a second plate. Lights were dim in the aircrew mess, a small and cluttered place, intimate, private, as if here only saints and angels sat. Always felt the same when I went in there. Uneasy. As if time had been borrowed and the loan was running out. As if the fellow beside you might be all but extinct. Did that include yourself?

Who started up the glamorous war myth? Goes a long way back. Back to Egypt. Back to Mesopotamia. Back to the Scriptures. Back to the Medes and Persians. What an infliction upon human youth. What an incredible disease of the human state.

At eleven—2300 hours by the air force clock—you were in the Operations Room to get the facts.

'It's this way, chaps. . . .'

A coal fire burning in the stove; a comfortable, lazy warmth in the place. Didn't seem quite right. Look after themselves in here, don't they? They don't have to walk out into the night, or be drenched by spray, or be terrified by flight. WAAFs flitting in and out, feminine, but indifferent to the comings and goings of aircrew tensed up. If a lad came through whom one might have loved never the flicker of an eyelid out of place. Nothing like the movies. No kisses round the corner as some intrepid youth tore himself away and took off.

You could hear those winds outside. So bleak. In here, shuffling of feet and senior officers and teacups and hard seats arranged one behind the other as if in church. Too much cigarette smoke. Too many poses. Too many squared jaws. Too many young fellows all rugged up trying to look fearless.

On the wall, a huge map. That much was like every film you ever saw of air force life. A huge map of the patrol zone—the Channel, the French coast, the Bay of Biscay, neutral Spain and neutral Portugal and the Atlantic wastes. Ribbons all over it. Done up like a maypole dance. Each ribbon was a patrol. One of them was yours. There were numbers and arrows signifying ships and their courses. There were areas where one was not permitted to bomb because British or American submarines were passing through them, en route. There were emblems for enemy aircraft and U-boats and warships and dinghies. (Long, long ago I was there looking at it, but see it clearer now than then.)

You were listening to voices, slow voices, deliberate, each stressing his point. Confusion crept in (for the new chum) and disquiet. So many do's. So many don't's. Strange and meaningless words took shape and hung in the air like musical notes. Code words with secret meanings—you didn't know what they were talking about. There sat the captain and his first pilot and his navigator and his senior wireless operator taking it all in as easily as arithmetical tables they had been learning since they were six. Or so you hoped. There were radio frequencies of great complexity and things called studs. There were Junkers 88's and Spanish destroyers and German U-boats. There were merchant vessels scattered in a gale. There were fishing vessels of every description all over the place. What was going on down there in the Bay? Sounded like late shopping night or the pre-Christmas rush. Out of their warm rooms came the briefing officers each to say his little bit. Back they went again to their warm rooms *to do what*?

'Good luck, chaps,' said the C.O. He was always there to say that, unless he was on leave, or sick, or had overslept. Bless me heart and soul I was there meself fourteen months later, Operations Officer, for a night. 'Good luck, chaps,' I said, and sent them off, joining the club, the Establishment Bloc.

Out into the cold and the dark and the wind. Oh my gosh. Struggling down to the pier, clumping laboriously, laden like a pack horse with equipment and rations and camera and binoculars and charts and homing pigeons and God alone knew what. Loaves of bread and drums of drinking water and chewing gum and Mars bars (one each) and letters from girls and photographs of girls and locks of hair and lucky charms and silver coins that had been kissed. (Did someone have a rabbit's foot?) When it was raining it was worse than that. Trying to keep everything dry. Trying not to get personally wet: sixteen hours ahead of you yet before you could change into anything else. Not funny sitting in an aircraft all those hours, freezing cold, wet.

Angle Bay came next. A pinnace was waiting at the pier to carry you there. Unsafe at night taking off in a Sunderland from Pembroke Dock. Too many hills, too close. In the black-out, risks were too huge to accept. So aboard you stepped and below you went through a heavy black curtain into a dimly lit place like a basement on the waterfront. The main cabin of the pinnace. Romantic, perhaps, in a historical sense.

There you sat, aware of each other, studiously, tediously appearing to be untroubled by the magnitude of events, while that pinnace purred six miles down harbour swaying like a hammock and you longed to fall asleep to escape. Not a word about flying. Not a word about war. Not a syllable said vivid enough to be drawn up to the top of the head. Every word said lost now in the subconscious deep.

Outside you had come to a point of arrival, to another significant step. Out there was the sea-plane tender, a substantial craft, moored at the end of the flare-path, and the pinnace was bumping against it. Squealing sounds of rubber gunwales, propellers under water whining in reverse (or something like that), voices of seamen, water slapping, wind in rigging, and the starred darkness of midnight waiting like a possessive acquaintance to encompass you. You groped up into the bleakness and the misery of it, yearning from your depths for warmth and for bed, wanting to go home, wanting to opt out, wanting to cuddle up in someone's arms, wanting to be mothered, I think.

The little dinghy was there, ready, bobbing, the coxwain's face upturned and dimly seen, and you stepped down from the pinnace into the lurching shell beneath, standing over to one side as pressure pushed you there, everybody crowding in shoulder to shoulder (how many will it take before it sinks?), everybody hugging equipment, everybody gathered like a grouped family portrait—faces strained and humourless; let's get it over with, they seemed to express.

A burst of engine in the dinghy's bowels and the motion

finds direction, north probably, or is it west? Bow lifting high like a chariot, stern sinking low, the whole thing like a fat horse. Astern, a profound surprise, something pulling at the spirit, to be seen for the first time, to be seen many times more, a turbulent and luminous wake lit with needles and sparkles of light, drawing the spirit and disturbing it. Wind is like ice on your cheeks, whipping up ruddiness for no one to observe, flecking eyes and lips with salt and spray, and ahead is a blackness, an unexplored void, a thousand million miles removed from where people are warm and human and sane. So cold out there.

Rubber squealing again: the dinghy's gunwales against the Sunderland's hull this time. You become accustomed to that also, but not yet; *now* it squeals along the edges of your nerves.

Lights go on inside the Sunderland; faint glimmers show around the blackout blinds. That's the duty hand, poor devil, groping out of his bunk, trying to waken and relate to the cock-eyed world. Where is he and what's he doing here? Why isn't he twelve thousand miles away secure in bed? He's a gunner left aboard the afternoon before at the end of the six-mile tow that had brought the Sunderland from Pembroke Dock to Angle Bay. The watch-dog left behind until the crew should arrive.

In the crew came, in they poured, bringing with them a roar of voices and wide-awakeness and me, feeling so *useless*, so genuinely scared, so genuinely in the way. There was nothing I was supposed to do; there was nothing I knew how to do. 'Make yourself familiar with things,' the captain said. 'That's all that's expected of you the first time. Wander as you please.'

Men (or boys) moving methodically through the drills of preparation; everything being done as 'laid down', always in the same order. 'Learn the drill like a parrot; say it over and over; go to sleep saying it; wake up saying it; it's your life you're learning to save.' Each going through his special drill for his special job; engrossed in the gloom. Miss a step of your particular drill and you become restless, ill-at-ease. 'What have I missed? Something's wrong.' Go back to the beginning and start another time.

Every man in his corner. Inspecting the bilges for leaks, pumping them dry; inspecting guns and ammunition and pyrotechnic supplies; adjusting the moorings to make ready for casting-off at the moment the captain calls; unlocking and testing the flying controls; arranging the signal colours in the sequence of the hours, those colours will be changing during patrol several times, fire the wrong cartridge when the Royal Navy is around and they'll give you every barrel up your tail; checking the cockpit, every instrument and lever, every switch and dial; checking the wireless, long and short wave; testing the engine controls and fuel lines; setting up the charts and navigation instruments; blacking out every porthole; groping outside along the wing to examine the mainplane for Heaven knows what, birds' nests maybe, or flying fish, or mermaids. Having something to do is good for a man.

How long does it take that night? Half a lifetime or half-an-hour—difficult to tell the difference at times. Then there's movement towards the bridge, fellows gathering there as if for a celebration of some sort, putting on life-jackets, tightening the tapes, some settling on the floor in the positions they'll occupy for take-off. The captain and first pilot going up front, through the blackout curtain, to sit, to strap in, to settle, to commit us finally to fate.

An engine exploding into life, sparks and fumes and smoke, the starboard outer I think, port outer soon following, and captain calling, 'Cast off.'

That's it. It's started. Your future belongs to luck. And you can't jump out, not when you swim like a brick.

Taxi-ing now, out into the harbour like a great lumbering bus, all engines running, spray cracking, waves thudding. Out there off the bow a long line of swaying little ships light up, the flare-path, the line along which you will take off. Running up the engines to clear the oil out, testing the ignition switches for magneto drop, checking for maximum take-off revs and boost, plunging wildly and unseeingly into the dark. They sure pile on the agony. Will I ever forget that night? Up and down the harbour. Back and forth. What on earth were they at? Why didn't they get on with it? Why didn't they take off? Didn't they know I was a nervous wreck? I wanted to get into the Bay of Biscay as fast I could get. All keyed-up to die. Waiting for it was worse than getting polished off.

They were cutting the inner engines. They were taxi-ing back. *They were mooring up.*

Engine performance was not good enough.

'No,' said the captain, 'I'm not taking off like that.'

Oh, the anguish. Having to live through your first trip twice. Next night having to perform, again, the same preliminary dance.

I can't be certain whether one *hardened* to the tension of operational flying or not. Perhaps, in time, the tension became its own anaesthetic. From a surfeit of fear you stopped being frightened. I don't know. For each man it was different.

But it was a hard way to learn a trade—in action. It was a long apprenticeship—in action. Perhaps your spirit seasoned like an old boot. Under the right kind of microscope it might even have looked like one.

When things were happening you coped. It was extraordinary how a run-of-the-mill coward could grow in seconds to meet bravely an enormous threat. But when nothing happened, when you flew for hours, patrol after patrol, expecting trouble at every minute, but meeting an endless empty space life became harrowing and grim. It was an awful way to spend your youth, all the time thinking: 'something's got to happen, something's got to happen, this kind of luck has got to break.' Yet some perverse streak permits you to remember it not wholly with distaste. It's the adventure you remember most. Somehow the sharp edges of the anguish and the confusion and the daunting moral issues fade out.

There was a danger area in the Bay, you soon learnt that, and it was at its worse to the east of ten degrees West. Tucked in behind that meridian and the coast of France there lay a very hot trouble zone for Sunderland flying-boats. . . .

Two U-boats had been seen by Wellingtons the night before, those Wellingtons with the searchlights in front. Aircraft of the night, specially equipped to attack in the dark. Were they also painted black? Did the Germans think of them as vampire bats? Dracula and all that? What was it like up there groping round the ocean night after night? Leigh Light Wellingtons, they called them, and it must have been a life! Bad enough in Sunderlands, in broad daylight.

Two U-boats and over fifty aircraft of Coastal Command and wireless signals of high priority humming in all directions and German fighter pilots in unknown numbers turned the Bay of Biscay that morning into a feverish kind of place. To be heading down into it was to be heading for something as surely as God made little ant-heaps. We were there in Sunderland S. Oh, yes.

The voice of the wireless operator came over the intercom. 'W/T to Captain. We have received a signal instructing us to fly to six degrees thirty minutes West, forty-four degrees North to search for a submarine. Fighter escort laid on.'

'Not to *us*?' said the captain. 'Not to us in person?'

'Yes, skipper.'

'Hell,' said the captain. (John was his name.) 'Six-thirty West! Two hundred miles in! We'll be dragging a wing over the French coast.'

'Yeh,' grumbled Control. 'Now listen to me, you blokes. You heard that; you couldn't miss. And you know what it means; you couldn't miss that either. We're going to be a mighty long way in, too far east to be turning west at the last minute and be hoping to get let off. If we're jumped, we're gone. You turrets keep your eyes peeled. You keep 'em popping against the perspex. What you'll be doing is looking for JU 88's. You'll be leaving the looking for U-boats to us on the bridge. Now I want acknowledgements. Okay, Tail, you first.'

'Tail to Control. Understood.'

'Midships to Control. Understood.'

'Nose to Control. Understood.'

'Galley to Control. Understood.'

'Right,' said Control. 'So start looking.'

The captain went skidding onto his new course. Almost due east. Unheard of, in broad daylight. If you ever had a nightmare that was the way it was—flying east towards France in broad daylight! *And now you were doing it in real life.* Has someone back at Base got a hate on us? Has some fellow back there got his eye on the captain's girl and reckons this is a sure way of knocking him out of the chase?

Brushing through the ragged cloud base. Thank God for clouds. Use them like bed-clothes. Tuck your head under the sheet. Grey water down there, splashes of sunlight, glaring brilliance, shadows like blots of ink. Gale-whipped white caps, columns of foam, long streaks of driven spray. Holy smoke. Ditch in that and you'll be dead in a wink.

Fighter escort, eh? That sounds all right. Never had fighter escort before, never seen anything in the Bay on a fighter aircraft looking anything like the roundels of the R.A.F. Seen plenty of black crosses though. Only last week. Gawd; how had we managed to live through that? These R.A.F. fighters, Mosquitoes maybe, or Beaufighters perhaps, will be rushing out into the hot zone in sixes and eights. Just like the 88's. Never tell the difference until they're screaming down your throat.

Morning coffee comes up to the bridge. Huge hunks of

bread with slabs of rough cheese in the middle. Ted's idea
of a sandwich; you get both hands on them then open your
mouth until your face splits. Ted's a little Scotsman with an
enormous personality—one of those R.A.F. fellows always
to be found about the place. Still not enough Australians to
fill all the crews and gap up the ranks. Not surprising. Six-
thirty West! They'd be more Australians short before
the sun set! What do you bet? How stupid could they
get? Six-thirty West. Might as well send you off to
bomb Berlin at a hundred and ten knots and a thousand
feet.

'Black coffee thanks, Ted. No sugar in it. Give it to me
thick and straight.'

First time, I think, I'd had black coffee in my life. Well,
first time I *almost* had it. Had the cup to my mouth when
down plunged the wing into a giddy turn to port.

'Captain to Galley. Open the bomb-doors. Run out the
bombs. Don't stop for breath.'

Whoosh. Down we went at a hundred and sixty knots.

'Dead ahead,' said the captain. 'Two miles in front.'

Standing up on the sea, a tall box of foam, looking like
a wardrobe or a conning-tower or anything you might like
to think up. Then the foam subsided and waves washed over
it and by the time we arrived nothing showed a trace. 'I'll
swear,' said the captain, 'that was a sub.'

'Are you sure it wasn't a white-cap?'

'Damned funny white-cap, mate.'

Course resumed. Bombs back in. Pulse rates slowing down
a bit. Ted mopping up the coffee and making another pot.
Wasn't difficult really. Coffee in a jiffy. Syrup in a bottle
that should never have been let out.

Flying on under cloud but the eastern horizon is a mass
of blazing light. Dark under the cloud. Mighty hard to see
up front. Anything approaching from France will come out
of the sun. *Beware the Hun in the Sun*. They used to stick it
up on notices all over the place. Along with 'Idle Talk Costs

Lives' and 'Coughs and Sneezes Spread Diseases, Trap the Germs in Your Handkerchief.'

Change of watch. Every hour change of watch used to come around. If you were lucky you might score some time off. More often than not you wriggled out of one place to wriggle at once into another. Unless you could manage to convince Control that if you did not spend five minutes in the lavatory en route you would not answer for the consequences. Terribly complicated business keeping a Sunderland in flight for fourteen hours straight.

Change of watch, of course. Everybody moving round in circles. Even the pilots changing seats. Even the captain managing to lean against the radio bulkhead to chew heavily on a mouthful of gum. Always the time to sight something. Always the time for some smart alec to switch on the intercom and report:

'Second Pilot to Control.' That's me. 'One aircraft on our port bow. Ten degrees. Same height. Range about twenty miles. I can see him glinting in the sun.'

'Captain to Second Pilot. You can see what? At how far? Incredible, boy. Get your glasses on it. It's probably Venus coming up.'

The captain hasn't known me long enough yet to realize that I have binoculars built in. That fear makes my eyes do extraordinary things. That I can practically see the Jerries taking off from their airfields below the horizon two hundred miles east. Through the glasses I see a tall tail fin. Like a flower-pot. 'It's a Sunderland, I think.'

'Remarkable,' says the captain. 'If you can see a Sunderland twenty miles off through that soup I reckon my middle name is Betty Grable.'

In the course of an hour the two Sunderlands are flying abreast about seven miles apart. The other fellow is F/461 and maybe our captain is reckoning his second pilot is psychic or something. 'Second Pilot to Control. There's another aircraft on the port beam now. Looks as though it's attacking F.'

Oh, that's great.

Oh, that's marvellous.

There it goes without a doubt, sweeping below the distant Sunderland and turning steeply near the water. It's on all right. Bush week. Sunderlands will be piling up all over the Bay before the day is out.

'How many engines has that aircraft got? Can you see it, Second Pilot?'

'Two engines. It's a Heinkel.'

'Midships here. It has four engines. It's a Liberator.'

'Nose here. Come off it. It's a Condor.'

'Condor be jiggered.'

'Control to all positions.' Sounding slightly pompous and slightly peeved. 'Dare I suggest a few lectures in aircraft recognition?'

'Captain to Control. Can you tell us what is it, please?'

'Haven't a clue.'

'Second Pilot to Captain. It's coming towards us.'

'Shall I turn, Control?'

'Can't be too hostile, Captain. Hasn't worried F. It's a Liberator, you know.'

It was, too.

Zoom. Straight across the Sunderland's bow not two hundred yards in front.

'Captain here. Holy cow. What is he at?'

'W/T to Captain. He's calling us up.'

'HE'S WHAT?'

'On the R/T, Captain. Plain language. With a strong American accent. He's asking us if we have any instructions for him.'

'ASKING?'

'Yes, Captain. The spoken word.' Poor W/T. That poor man. Sounding as if everything he has believed in has been proved to be false. 'What shall I tell him, Captain?'

'TELL HIM? DAMN HIM! DOES HE THINK I'M THE BRAINS TRUST? OF COURSE I HAVEN'T

ANY CRIMSON INSTRUCTIONS. DOES HE WANT
HELL SHOT OUT OF THE LOT OF US? HASN'T HE
HEARD OF RADIO SILENCE?'

Whereupon the captain borrows a cigarette and the second
pilot lights it for him. And the captain sits there with his
chest heaving and his shoulders rising and falling and with a
face as ashen as a face can get.

S drones on sedately.

More fun. Ted is in the tail. Never any doubt when Ted
is in the tail. He's always left something behind. 'Tail to
Control. Beg pardon. Tail to Galley I mean. . . .' Utter
Dutch following. Scottish brogue degenerating (if degenera-
tion be possible) into a meaningless gabble of animal
sounds. Then comes silence and Ted switches off. Silence
hanging most heavily in the earphones, everyone non-
plussed. Then from the galley comes another Scottish voice—
Jock, the Aberdonian engineer. 'Okay, Tail. I'll get it for
you.'

The captain wrings his hands.

Farther south. Farther east. Nearer Jordan. Hear dem
angels singing.

Broken cloud. Scattered rain. Sunshine. Black shadows.
Patches of blue sky. High seas. Spume. Pounding hearts.
Blood thundering in temples. Exquisite racking strain.
Flying in along the forty-fourth parallel. Here comes the
Sunderland. Here come the supermen. Here come the
Aussies. Out of the way you JU 88's or you might go shooting
us down.

'Should see the Beaufighters pretty soon, I reckon,' says
Control.

'Yeh. Hope so.'

'If they're here.'

'Meaning?'

'Anything you like to think. . . .'

First pilot up front in the captain's seat is searching with
his binoculars around the port beam and his voice comes

cracking into the intercom with the kind of urgency he
reserves for disasters. 'First Pilot to Control. Three aircraft
on the port bow, eighty degrees, moving on to the beam.
Range fifteen miles. Below us by a couple of hundred feet.
Almost on the deck. Almost whipping up the spray.'

'*Three* aircraft. What sort of aircraft?'

'Twin-engined. Going like hell.'

'Oh—'

Panic.

First pilot hurtling out of the left-hand seat, captain
replacing him. Second pilot hurtling out of the right-hand
seat, first pilot replacing him. Captain poking his forefinger
in the air for LOTS of power, first pilot giving it to him.
Control springing into his astrodome and declaring,
'Can't see 'em. Can't see 'em. Where are they?' Turrets
can't see a thing. Bridge can't see a thing. First pilot hasn't
a clue where to look any longer. *Where are those aircraft?*

Chewing at gum like crazy. Fingers looking white round
the knuckles. Knees like all the bones down there have
turned mushy. Won't get away with it this time. Four
88's last week but that was dead lucky. Three this week is
just the right number. Missing . . . presumed killed. Can't
you see it in print? Weeping families. Maidens in black.
Pay-day tomorrow. Oh Lord, preserve my wicked body.

'Captain here. Watch the clouds, you fellows; for Pete's
sake keep your eyes on them. They'll jump us as sure as a
chicken.'

Yeh. That's fine and dandy. But you're still going east.
Fly west, young man.

'Tail to Control. Just saw an aircraft through the clouds.
About six miles.'

'Watch it.'

'Can't see it now.'

'Still watch.'

'Tail to Control. There it is again.'

'Keep an eye on it!'

'It's flying away. It's heading away. It's gone.'

Thank Heaven for small mercies.

Very deep sigh.

Peace again.

Still flying east. On to 7° 40′ . . . 7° 20′ . . . knocking on the door of 7° 00′ west. . . .

Dinner turns out to be most uninteresting though cooked with such labour down on the bottom deck. Can't swallow very well; is that what the trouble is? Can't do anything very well except shake.

Clouds are looking thicker. . . . Please, God, do you reckon you could send us a solid mass, say, from sea level to ten thousand feet? We must be getting into the country where Jerry fighters are lined up in battalions.

'First Pilot to Control.' (I wish that fellow would shut-up.) 'Aircraft ahead. Up two thousand feet in the blue patch.'

Up leaps every eye on board like a well-drilled troop, but nothing is there. For ten seconds nothing but the blue patch, then into it with cloud streaming from his wingtips comes the Gentleman from America in his Liberator bus.

'Control to Captain. We have reached six degrees thirty minutes West.'

'Thank you,' says the captain, in a hollow-type voice.

Nothing out there to see, though. Even the Liberator has vanished. No fighters out there, friendly or hostile, no submarines, and no horizon. There's a haze out there at least a thousand feet deep. Is that going to work in our favour or against us?

'Control to Captain. I'd say we ought to be seeing things by now. Perhaps we could start searching?'

'Yeh.'

So we head north, then west, then south. Nothing is there but abstracts, nothing but invisible forces, nothing but billions of little fear cells rushing in diminishing circles with us in the middle. Then we head east again as if the agony isn't enough without making it worse. Not a sign of those

Beaufighters. Never did see a friendly fighter, that day or any other day. Maybe there weren't any. Ever.

Cloud masses start breaking up. Blue sky and sunlight and bright ocean patches breaking out all over like a horrible rash. Worse than walking naked up the middle of Main Street. Here come those Junkers. What do you bet! Here come all those German fellows to polish us off. So what do I go and do? See something at that crucial moment. 'Second Pilot to Control.' Saying it with great deliberation, lots of time being necessary to get each word shaped without choking to death from fright. 'There is an object on the water eighty degrees on the port bow. Range fifteen miles, I guess. You can see it in a patch of sunlight. It's just got to be a U-boat, I guess.'

That really stirs 'em up. Bodies rushing all over the place. People leaping in and out of seats to make sure the best man is in the proper spot. Second pilot staying put, for once, in the right-hand seat, with binoculars up to his face though he always manages to see straighter and farther without their use. Still no comment coming from anywhere else.

'Captain here. I'm waiting for some confirmation. Who can see it?'

Not a sound on the intercom. Not even a deep breath.

'Second Pilot to Captain. It's still where I said. Port bow. Eighty degrees. Maybe twenty miles. It's a heck of a long way off. Turn to port a bit. Yeh, like that. Dead ahead. Strike me, I can see it without the glasses. Right in front. Three patches of sunlight. Take the middle one. Dead in the centre of it. Gawd, it's practically waving at us.'

'Can't see a sausage,' says Control. 'Can't see a U-boat either. You've got hallucinations, mate.'

'Second Pilot to all positions.' Sounding even more deliberate. Getting a wee bit cross. 'Use the sun-splashes like I said. As a reference. Plumb in the middle of the second splash.'

'Captain to Turrets. *You* watch the sky. *We'll* handle the sub, if there is one, from the Bridge.'

Pause. Young Southall taking a mighty sniff. 'Maybe it's twenty-five miles. Backing round on to the bow. Seventy degrees. Stone the crows. Is every blighter blind?'

'Captain to Galley. Put the stove out. Open the bomb-doors. Get someone to man the nose gun. Something must be there.'

Sweeping round through the clouds. Beautiful clouds for peeping through and hiding behind. 'Still there. Forty-five degrees port now. Sticking out in that sunlight like a colonial.'

'Control to Second Pilot. Are you Arthur or are you Martha? What the hell does it look like?'

'A sub standing beam on. Like the conning-tower. Gawd, you can't miss it. As plain as the nose on your face.'

'I don't know,' grumbles Control. 'What's he got in his head? Eyes or imagination? I can't see a flipping thing.'

Boring into cloud and turning head-on to the target. Depth-charges quivering on the racks. Everybody's nerves dancing to the music. Out again into the open. Nothing in sight to the ends of creation. Second pilot grumbling to himself about stupid people too slow to catch a cold and too blind to see a wall until they walk into it. More cloud and more clear. Sun-splashes gone. Everything gone. U-boat crash dived, of course, to safety. What a shockin' waste of opportunity.

'Tail to Control.' Jubilation seems to be the sound that's coming from the rear end. Second pilot sitting up and taking notice. 'Something on the waterrr. Port quarter. Ten degrees. Eight miles.'

Justification! Is it glorious, beautiful justification? Now we'll be seeing who's Arthur or Martha.

Round goes the captain, asking no questions, accepting the word of that Scotsman without hesitation (implying further dubious reflections upon the second pilot), screaming his Sunderland through a hundred and seventy degrees, thrusting down the nose, winding up the engines, everything howling and shaking, bursting out into the open leaving cloud high above him.

'Bejabbers,' says Control, forgetting he's not Irish. 'It's there and no doubt about it.'

All of it. Stuck out in the middle of a lone ray of sunshine, all silvery and brilliant and spotlessly sparkling. But what in thunder is it?

'Nose to Control. Never seen anything like it. Is it a balloon?'

'Could be,' says the captain, 'that's a reasonable supposition. Possibly a decoy. I've been reading about them. The U-boats let them go before they go plunging down under. Push 'em out in dozens to muck up our radar.'

'Don't think they pushed this one out, skipper. It's as big as a house, this one.'

'Second Pilot to Control. Looks to me like the wreckage of an aircraft.'

'Doesn't look like that to anyone else, kid. You're still seeing double.'

'Captain to Control. It's got to be a balloon. Can't be anything else. But certainly too big for a decoy.'

Over the top of it. Zoom! Round and round it.

A barrage balloon.

I mean, *a barrage balloon.*

Hundreds of miles from anywhere, half in the water and half out of it. Half collapsed. Half submerged. Where in the name of glory had it come from? Deported from Plymouth?

'All right,' says Control, 'so we have to admit it. The kid saw something. Now there are matters of somewhat greater urgency. Course for base, Captain. A direct course I'm suggesting. There seems to have been a miscalculation. Could we have overstayed our endurance a little? Thanks to the second dickey and his blasted balloon. But it's nothing to worry about.'

'Nothing, Control? *Absolutely* nothing to worry about?'

'Well—if we jettisoned our depth-charges and threw out surplus equipment and wasted no more time discussing it and set course for the Scilly Isles we might just make it. Or fly direct to France and surrender.'

'Thank you, Control. Is *that* all?

'Your course is 348 degrees compass.'

So the captain starts turning, sighing heavily, and calls up the galley. 'Captain to Galley,' he says, sort of stiffly. 'Open the bomb-doors and run out the depth-charges for jettisoning. I'm descending to a hundred feet.'

When he gets to a hundred feet he says, 'Are you ready, Galley?'

'Bomb racks out, skipper.'

Finger on the button, poised. Interruption!

'Tail to Control.'

'What is it, Tail?'

'May I fire a few rounds when you drop the bombs?'

Pause: of the kind known as pregnant.

'Control here. Did I hear you right?'

'Please may I fire a few rounds when the captain drops the bombs?'

'In the name of all that's holy! WHAT FOR?'

'To relieve the monotony.'

'MONOTONY! SPLIT ME! YOU'D BETTER TURN YOUR——GUNS THIS WAY, TED! I'M COMING DOWN TO KILL YOU!'

Uneventful patrol. That's what we said it was when finally we got home. What else could you have called it? Nothing happened worth reporting.

CHAPTER NINE

The Great Combat

This is one of the great and tragic stories of the Second World War. The Chief of Air Staff, R.A.F., said it would 'go down to history'. It has.

It is a combat in the 'great' and ancient traditions of combat, and as such I have told it without embellishment; a vast, violent, terrible and overwhelming story of enormous courage against enormous odds.

By now you know (or did I forget to tell you?) that the Sunderland was a converted airliner, first designed in the early nineteen-thirties for the long air-routes of the world and adapted for war-time use by the obvious addition of three turrets, nose, midships and tail, a total standard armament of seven .303 machine-guns. The largest 'shell' its standard armament could fire would have passed through the barrel of an infantryman's rifle. Squadron modifications—to increase that armament—turned up from time to time. Colin Walker's aircraft, Sunderland N, had an extra .303 machine-gun firing from each of the two galley hatches. That was all in the way of extras N took that June day down into the Bay of Biscay to do battle with eight Junkers 88's. The 88 was a superb aircraft, a twin-engined heavy fighter, much faster than the Short Sunderland, and much more heavily armed. Each 88 had a crew of four and an armoury of fixed and free-firing cannons and heavy-calibre machine-guns.

The Sunderland and the 88 were long-standing enemies; odds favoured the 88, yet again and again the Sunderland performed against large formations with distinction. The Germans called the Sunderland 'The Flying Porcupine'— apparently under the misapprehension that it bristled with guns. There seems to me to be only one explanation for the remarkable success achieved by the Sunderland; quality of aircraft and quality of men. After Walker's combat, after events had been weighed, the Sunderland became the inspiration of a German intelligence report. This report stated that the Sunderland's armour-plated hull deflected cannon-shells, and its secret weapon, allegedly a 37mm. gun, was used with devastating effect. Its heaviest weapon in fact was rifle-gauge and its hull was duralumin as thin as card.

That day Walker had a crew of eleven including himself. Dowling was his first pilot, Amiss was his second pilot. Simpson was his navigator and fire controller. Miles and Turner were the engineers. Fuller, Miller, Lane, Watson and Goode were the wireless operators and air gunners. They had flown together for a fair length of time, they knew each other and understood each other, and had survived a savage and dangerous combat with 88's and FW-190's several months before. Time may have worked for Sunderland crews by helping each man to identify closer with the spirit that made the crew. It worked that way, I think, until crews became tired. Life then was very dangerous and likely to be short. Walker and his boys had not reached that stage.

At briefing they heard of a British civil aircraft flying home from Gibraltar that had met a large formation of JU 88's over the bay. Everybody was het-up about it; the airliner had been shot down apparently with the loss of all lives. An unarmed and undefended British airliner. Slaughtered, was the word. But it was wartime, and if unarmed and undefended British aircraft flew that route perhaps it was the fault of the British, not of the Germans, when aircraft failed to arrive. Twelve passengers and crew had gone to their deaths, the actor Leslie Howard amongst them, yet probably all died from a case of mistaken identity. It seems that the Luftwaffe was under the impression that a very high ranking Allied leader, possibly Churchill, was aboard. They quickly learnt of their mistake and went hunting for the next likely-looking aeroplane to come by. (Sunderlands were often used for V.I.P. transportation.) Walker, in the meantime, was asked to search for survivors. Hence Walker and the 88's flew converging courses and met for the most incredible air combat ever fought over those seas. Vengeance was taken in awful terms. An eye for an eye and a tooth for a tooth, to a man. And again the Germans were mistaken, because Winston Churchill was not aboard the Sunderland either, and the extraordinary ferocity of the German attack became curiously pointless, almost a death wish.

The weather at Pembroke Dock was dull and the Sunderland flew south into drizzling rain that went sweeping across a dreary sea. Cloud was low and forced the aircraft low and it wasn't much like summer in Australian terms. The port-inner engine was misbehaving, fluctuating and spluttering, and every now and then squirting flame from the exhausts, irritating Walker and keeping him sharply alert. Farther south sun-rays began to break through and areas of misty brightness lay between cloud and sea. Walker crept up to a couple of thousand feet and visibility gradually extended, but the engine went on spitting and spluttering hour after hour, straining not only his patience but his sense of caution as well. Engine trouble was a peculiar and contrary irritation. If you returned to Base you could be certain it would get better. If you pressed on, it usually became worse. So what were you supposed to do?

'Captain to Engineer,' Walker said. 'This engine, Ted. What do you think? What is it going to do to us?'

Miles said, 'I'd give it thirty minutes, Captain. If it hasn't cleared then I'd consider turning back.'

'All right. Thirty minutes.' And that would be long enough. Five and a half hours out from Base. Five and a half hours to get back!

It was 1835, Greenwich time, change of watch, and most of the crew were on the move. The change brought Walker back to the flying seat and first pilot Dowling to the right-hand seat. It put Goode in the Tail, Fuller up in Midships, and Watson down in the Nose. Turner relieved Miles at the engineer's bench and Miles went down to the galley to start brewing tea. Miller found himself at the wireless and Simpson as usual made no move. One navigator/fire-controller only. Thirteen, fourteen, fifteen hours straight he had to work unrelieved, unaided, the hardest-worked man aboard and the one whose function was the most critical. He never won the captain's glory but there was little any captain could do without him.

Simpson stood now in the astrodome and looked over a glaring sea and cloudless sky. All mist had gone, every cloud had melted away, every shadow like a washed-out stain had disappeared. Always the same. Set a foot in the danger zone and there you were, stuck out like a pimple on the end of your nose. Every way you looked there you were, part of every view, on your splendid own, visible from the ends of the world.

'Control to all positions. I remind you of our briefing. Keep a sharp look-out. We're in Tiger Country now and yesterday, not far from here, the airliner went down. We'll pass directly over the position where the attack began. So watch out for dinghies please.'

On to 1845 and the sea heaved gently down there. It was almost calm, its surface marked mainly by long curving ripple lanes made by breezes. There might have been haze softening the tones. There might have been U-boats creeping westward beneath the surface. There might have been dead men no one could see. This was combat country, far from parachutes to swing you to land, far from patriots in the back country to help you home; far, far away you were, on your own. Great white Sunderland. Ocean bird. Sun blazing hot, still hours high. No man of any sensitivity flew through there without fear, sometimes.

1900 hours, Greenwich time, June 2, 1943.

'Tail to Control.' A sharp and urgent voice. 'Eight air-aircraft. Thirty degrees on the port quarter. Six miles. Up one thousand feet.'

The sort of thing that started your head running wild. . . .

Simpson leapt back to the astrodome. Walker rammed his throttles wide and sounded the klaxon horn, the alarm signal that sent every man off watch racing for the nearest socket to plug in his earphones. Dowling hauled on the pitch levers and engines howled at twenty-six hundred revolutions a minute, all the power they had.

'Control to Tail. Can you identify those aircraft?'

'Twin-engined,' said Goode. 'Probably Junkers 88's.'

That was what they were and in they came.

'Captain to W/T.' Walker's voice was as calm as he could make it sound. That was his particular responsibility just then; the untroubled demeanour while the world was falling down. 'Message to Group. O/A Priority. Attacked by eight JU 88's. . . . How's that inner engine, Engineer?'

'The same.'

'Captain to Galley. Are the bomb-racks out?'

'Ready, Captain.'

Walker's thumb squeezed the button. 'Right. Bombs gone. Now you've got to work fast. Run in the racks, close the door and get cracking with the galley gun installations. Who's down there to man them?'

'Miles on the starboard, sir. Lane on the port.'

'Control to all positions.' That was Simpson again. 'They've spread out around us and I want you to hold fire until they're in range. No waste please. No shooting before six hundred yards. Three have gone to the starboard beam, three to the port beam, and one to each quarter. Range fifteen hundred yards, fifteen hundred feet up.'

134

And there they paused, poised.

The seconds dragged.

'Control to all positions. . . . I think they're coming. . . . Yes, here they are. One peeling off from each beam. Prepare to corkscrew. Twelve hundred yards. One thousand yards. They're firing. Prepare to corkscrew. Starboard is leading. Eight hundred yards. Corkscrew starboard. GO!'

Walker jammed the wheel over with a violent thrust of strength and the Sunderland screwed steeply down with shell and tracer fire blasting through it.

'Corkscrew port. NOW TO THE PORT. PORT. GO!'

Walker savagely reversed controls and the Sunderland shuddered to the awful shock and climbed giddily to the left, the pressures crushing crew-men into their seats or into the deck, Simpson hanging desperately to his holding place to avoid being torn by gravity out of the dome.

The port-outer engine broke into flame, and smoke and fire went scattering like shreds of fabric over the wing. Incendiary bullets ripped into the cockpit and Walker's compass blew up like a small bomb, erupting showers of blazing alcohol. Fire, like something alive, sprayed over Walker and splashed across the bridge and went pouring down the companionway into the bow compartment. Sound and vibration and choking smoke and terrifying little tongues of fire ran through the cockpit and somewhere a voice in the confusion was urging Walker to straighten his controls, to level out; Simpson saying, 'Straighten up, straighten up. They're coming again. Two more on the way.' And second pilot, Amiss, almost blinded by smoke, was wrenching the fire extinguisher from the bracket on the bulkhead and turning it full onto his captain, because Walker was burning.

'Eight hundred yards,' Simpson was saying. 'Prepare to corkscrew port.'

Walker yelled at Dowling, 'Fly her. Take over. We've got to put out these fires.'

Fly West

In came the 88's, screaming in for the kill, on to the Sunderland gushing smoke.

'Corkscrew port. GO.'

Fire and extinguishing fluid and smoke and Walker half-suffocated in the midst of it, but somehow Dowling was still flying her, blindly, by instinct, plunging giddily down, responding to Simpson's voice. Amiss, trying to get those fires out, could scarcely stand up, was thrown from bulkhead to bulkhead and crushed into the deck, spraying fluid at every flame he could reach. Walker got his hand to the Graviner switch to extinguish the blazing engine and the port outer wing section seemed to turn into a cloud of dense white smoke, trailing and curving through the sky like a signal foreshadowing death. All power from that engine ceased and the airscrews windmilled and dragged like a mass of bricks, throwing an enormous strain on Dowling's skill and strength while he wound, almost with desperation, on the trimming tabs, trying to take some of the pressure off.

Simpson's voice was droning on. 'Corkscrew starboard. Corkscrew starboard. They're still coming. . . .' But trying to turn to the right against the drag of the dead engine was almost beyond strength and beyond reach.

Walker was yelling at Amiss. 'Give the wireless operator a message for Group, "On Fire".'

In came the 88's in alternating pairs, pressing home their attacks to point-blank range, filling the air through which the Sunderland reeled with incendiaries and explosives and shrapnel showers, while Dowling jiggled with throttles and thrusts at his rudder to swing the great boat round.

'Straighten up. Straighten up. . . .' A drop came in the pitch of Simpson's voice. 'A breather. A breather. They're reforming. Returning to the quarters and the beams.'

Seconds to catch breath, to adjust. Seconds during which Walker resumed the controls and Amiss got the fires out. Seconds to realize that they were in trouble. No escape from this lot. No hope of fighting this one through. That was how

136

it looked. Hope was one thing; impossibilities were another. Shot full of holes, an engine gone, Walker injured, eight 88's still riding proud and high. 'We've got this game sewn up.' You could almost hear the German airmen singing. But someone else was singing; Fuller in the midships turret, that English lad, way up there on top in the weakening sunlight singing a popular song of the day:

'*Praise the Lord and pass the ammunition,*
Praise the Lord and pass the ammunition.'

What did Walker think about that? The young voice in the intercom that Simpson had to shout over:

'They're coming!'

No more singing just then, just a boy's deep breath, and Simpson's voice coming in again, calmly and strong. 'One from port and one from starboard. As before. Firing from a thousand yards. We'll go starboard first. Eight hundred yards. Starboard's clearly in front. Turn and dive starboard. GO!

'Tighter than that. Tighter. PORT. CORKSCREW PORT. He's coming right in. Tight as you can make it, Col. TIGHTER.'

Walker fighting with his controls, all but beyond his strength, shells and bullets crashing into the Sunderland along the port side, Goode back in the tail, where gravity was like a merry-go-round, firing when he could at the 88 on the port side flashing in, but Fuller was letting it go, letting it come, his two guns fully depressed, his turret turned off to starboard, Simpson thinking he was dead.

There rested Fuller (about twenty years of age), resting on his guns, head down, barrels down, eyes slitted, watching bullet holes spatter all around, watching the 88 on the starboard side hurtle at him, watching it grow, watching it loom above him, filling the sky, head-on, fifty yards point blank.

Up flashed Fuller's guns, up they whipped, sighted and shooting and hundreds of rounds poured into the 88 as it broke away, slaughtering it, cutting it in bits, exploding it into flame and fragments and ballooning black smoke. Down it went vertically, screaming into the sea.

Fuller was singing:

'*Praise the Lord and pass the ammunition. . . .*'

'Straighten up. Straighten up.'

That was Simpson calling, Simpson, not unmoved.

'Get some height, Col. Get as much as you can. They're coming again. A variation. Two in line astern on the port quarter. Twelve hundred yards. Prepare to turn and dive to port. One thousand yards and they're firing cannon. Turrets, wait on my order. Eight hundred yards. Turn and dive to port. Turrets, hold fire. PORT. GO!'

Over they went and down, down in a tightening turn towards the sea, no man firing except the leading JU 88, Walker tightening the turn more and more, increasing the stresses, straining his nerves, no one firing except that 88, Simpson not saying a word, shells and armour-piercing bullets shredding the Sunderland's hull, shooting away the elevator and rudder trimming wires, severing the hydraulic lines to the tail turret which slammed destructively against its stops, knocking Goode senseless.

On went Walker, screaming round his turn, no Sunderland gunner firing a shot, Simpson still not uttering a word, the first 88 breaking away, the second coming in, rushing in to two hundred yards.

'FIRE!' bawled Simpson.

They fired, Nose and Midships together, Fuller and Watson as one man, and off went the tracers, three lines of tracers, spinning a lazy arc into the Junkers' heart. It pulled up sharply, as if leaping an obstacle, a positive movement as it broke away. After it went Fuller and Watson, firing without pause into its belly. A thin stream of smoke snaked from the 88's starboard engine, then a gush of dark, ugly flame. It dropped, as if lift had been taken away, and struck the sea in a huge plume of foam. Almost like a ball it bounced and hung for an instant, then plunged down. A column of oily smoke went up from its grave as if a rocket had been fired.

'*Praise the Lord and pass the ammunition,*
Praise the Lord and pass the ammunition.'

The boy went on singing his tune and over him Simpson said, 'Superb. Superb. Two destroyed, Colin. . . . There's another coming now on the starboard. Prepare to turn and dive to starboard. . . .'

Walker turned, shouting to Amiss who stood there, clinging to the bulkhead. 'Get another message away. "Two shot down"!'

Amiss lurched back.

'Turn and dive to starboard. GO!'

'And now they're coming from below. Targets here for you, Galley. Watch them there. One on each quarter. Fire as soon as you can. Tail, there's a target for you. Get into him. Good shooting, Galley. You've scared him away. That 88 on the starboard is still coming in. I want to see your fire, Tail!

'Control to Tail. . . .

'Control to Captain. Something's happened to Tail.'

'Captain to Second Pilot. Get him out and put a galley gunner in. Be quick.'

'New attack from the starboard. Coming in ahead. One thousand yards on the starboard bow. Two aircraft in line astern. Prepare to corkscrew starboard. Eight hundred. CORKSCREW. GO!'

Something burst. Something exploded in their midst. A cannon-shell on the bridge, against the radio bulkhead. Shrapnel pieces and splintering glass and acrid smoke, petrol gauges shattering, every instrument in sight fracturing, flesh breaking into blood, the wireless failing, wrecked, in the middle of the message. Miller, the operator, was injured. Dowling was injured. Simpson was injured. Miles, below on the starboard galley gun, was mortally injured, and collapsed.

Simpson, too, collapsed, with a lump of shrapnel in his leg and had to drag himself up into the dome again to try to peer out. In that instant the 88 went over the top and Simpson tried to resume his commentary, but couldn't hear his voice. There was no feedback. Nothing. The intercom was dead.

A long moment of dreadful confusion, Walker sensing he was on his own, and somehow wrenching the Sunderland out of its turn though it did not want to respond. Chaos. Twisted metal and broken glass. Cordite reeking. Walker's muscles almost tearing at the controls. No intercom. No wireless. No airspeed indicator. Airframe warped, the whole aeroplane twisted out of shape. Felt like a steam engine. Felt as heavy as one. Felt as manoeuvrable as one. Walker shaking his head and glancing out to port. An incredible sight. *That instant.* Off fell the port-outer propellers and their reduction gear; off they fell from the engine and tumbled into the sea. And out there an 88 was coming in, burning in, spraying its bullets already from short range. Desperately, Walker turned towards it, calling out of himself all his strength and shouting for Dowling to help him round. Together they managed it, coordinating, somehow they turned, and over the top went the 88 and underneath went the Sunderland.

Simpson was still in the dome, frustrated, his voice silenced, his function defeated. What the pilots saw they might possibly avoid. What they did not see would shoot them down. 'Help me,' Simpson screamed at Miller, pointing to the cockpit. 'Watch me. Tell them what to do.'

Miller struggled up forward to stand between the pilots, bracing himself there against all the pressures of evasive action and the pain of his wounds, mimicking the movements that Simpson was making in the dome, Simpson flying the evasive action with his hands and his screaming voice, with his life-blood oozing over his boots.

Below, in the galley, Miles was dying. Amiss and Lane

lifted him clear of his gun and tried to take him through to the wardroom, to make him comfortable there, but the wardroom door would not open. They tried to force it, but it would not move. No door that was shut ever opened again; no door that was open was it possible to close, so greatly was the airframe twisted. They laid Miles on the lurching bomb-room floor and Turner came down from the engineer's bench to man the gun and the air was still full of smoke and fire and shrapnel and stinking explosives.

Walker and Dowling were flying together, muscle to muscle, reflex to reflex, flying with incredible precision an aircraft which was scarcely an aircraft any longer, still turning, still corkscrewing, still diving into every developing attack with all the power their three grossly abused engines could give them. Again and again and again the 88's attacked with baffling ferocity.

Amiss was on his way to the tail. Had to get Goode out. Had to put someone in his place. For Heaven's sake, who? Couldn't leave the tail unmanned. That was the big sting—four guns up there. Take away the tail and how could you survive? How had they survived until now? There was the mystery. Fighting back with pea-shooters. Somehow staying aloft. Amiss down on all fours like an animal, clinging to the catwalk, fighting his way aft an inch at a time, covered from head to foot in oil and muck and de-icing fluid from punctured tanks and hydraulic lines, Amiss getting rammed from side to side with the violence of flight, the hull around him like a tattered curtain, gaping and torn. How would he get Goode out, for Heaven's sake? He was scared he would fall out himself before he arrived. Great rents from cannon explosions, multitudinous holes from machine-gun spray. Goode would be torn apart.

So Amiss got there, the turret, down on all fours, shaken and sickened and stunned. He could see the sky out there and the sea sweeping and weaving. He could see 88's out there through holes in the Sunderland's hull. The turret was jammed over to port, as far as it could go, and Goode was hunched in a heap. Amiss crashed his fist against the turret door, repeatedly, as if to say, 'Wake up.' As if to say, 'Let me in.' Incredibly, he realized he was looking into living eyes and Goode was giving him a sick grin and turning up his thumbs. *Incredible.* Goode was shocked and concussed and confused but stubbornly not interested in vacating his turret. Amiss tried to get him out, but Goode wouldn't move. He shook his head at Amiss, pushed him away, and snapped out of shock and began to operate his turret with body pressure and to trip his guns with his fingers. Even while Amiss watched, clinging for a handhold in the shattered tail, Goode started fighting back.

On the bridge, in conditions of unbelievable material disorder, Walker and Dowling and Simpson and Miller controlled their fate with a calm and a discipline that almost defeats human explanation. Burnt and bloodied and wounded, all four men remained totally in command of themselves and of the situation. Their calm grew. Their confidence expanded. They *would* achieve the unbelievable. They *would* survive this thing. It seems they must have *willed* it. Or was someone at prayer for them? I don't know. Did the 88's know? I don't know that either.

There came a pause, a distinct and definite pause, and the 88's withdrew to the beams and the quarters to reform. Six 88's bent on vengeance, resolute for blood. How many times had they attacked already? Fifteen times? Twenty times? Does anyone know? Could anyone be sure now, or then?

They came. In they came for the final assault, for the ultimate kill, one 88 leading from the starboard quarter. Simpson again beginning to act his pantomime, Miller to mimic it, Walker and Dowling to put it into effect with a steep diving turn to starboard that they reversed in time to meet another attack coming from the port. Fuller broke the attack on the starboard side, his long-range tracer scaring the enemy off, but the 88 on the port side was hell bent. In it came fiercely, holding its dive, holding its approach, and Goode got his sights on it, holding his turret steady with physical strength, depressing the sears of his guns with his fingers, and sending his tracers ripping into the great jutting engines. At point-blank range young Fuller whipped up his guns and poured two hundred rounds into its belly and away screamed the 88 as if agonized, in a crazy blazing arc, and smashed into the sea at three hundred miles an hour.

They came again, those German airmen, and again, and again, driven by rage or desperation or pride, or unthinking dedication. Each attack was broken. Around that Sunderland was a shield, an aura of courage, an irresistable will to live. It it true that in the history of German operations in the Bay of Biscay no other body of fighters ever met such phenomenal gunnery. Not one escaped undamaged. No other body of fighters in that zone ever suffered a defeat so shattering.

Another onslaught—seemingly of suicidal intent. In it came to point-blank range across the starboard bow but its crew could not bring a gun to bear. Outwitted and outmanoeuvred, there it hung exposed to Watson in the nose. He poured a can of ammunition into its port wing and it vanished, engine on fire, black smoke blooming from the cockpit, and God alone knows where it went or where it ended. And the world changed then.

Tension seemed to pass from the sky and two 88's only remained.

There they sat off the port beam two thousand yards out, flying with the Sunderland, aghast, confounded, demoralized, *yet they came again.*

One behind the other they came on to the beam, but someone must have said: 'Are we mad? Let's cut and run.' At eight hundred yards, not a shot fired, the attack collapsed, the will broke, they veered east and headed home.

The sky emptied. N/461 flew alone, position unknown.

Walker throttled back his shuddering engines and his speed fell away and in a circle, a slow circle, his groaning aircraft went round and round and round.

The engines beat their strange, tormented sound, shreds of metal flapped and clapped, wind cried and whined, but no man spoke a word.

Silence. Deep breathless pain. Men white and bloodless, violently trembling. Lips black, as if beaten and bruised. Tongues swollen to grotesque proportions in their mouths. Sweat pouring from them. Their spirits crying.

Walker said a prayer, inside.

But no man spoke a word aloud.

They knew that this was *special time*.

Seven thousand rounds expended by the Sunderland.

Three JU 88's destroyed.

One JU 88 probably destroyed.

Four JU 88's damaged, one of them possibly failing to reach home.

The British naval listening station, maintaining its constant watch over German frequencies, listening in wonder to repeated calls directed to the formation of JU 88's . . . What had those 88's run into? A cataclysm? Only two replied.

What of No 19 Group Headquarters Coastal Command on Plymouth Hoe? What of Pembroke Dock and the squadron there? Walker was believed lost. The signal cut short by the exploding cannon-shell was read as his last. Three aircraft were at once diverted to search. They found only patches of oil on the water.

Somewhere in the Bay of Biscay, God knew where, Walker set a course that he hoped might find England, then the pilots moved round, Dowling to the left-hand seat, Amiss to the right-hand seat, and Walker to step back and away. Walker to stand for a while, to stretch, to grow calm. It all took time.

Dowling and Amiss flew together, Dowling with his hands to the wheel, both men with their feet to the rudder bar. That was to be Amiss's role for hours more of agony, his special role, *all* his weight against the rudder bar to assist Dowling to hold the aircraft straight. When the strain became unendurable, when the nerves in his legs were breaking for relief, he bent beneath the panel and dragged on the bar with his hands.

On the bomb-room floor Miles died.

Walker sat Simpson on the navigation table and looked him over. His trousers were sodden with blood, his boots were covered in blood. If you're not used to that sort of thing it's not easy to look at and not easy to put up with. They snipped his trousers at the seams and ripped them apart up the legs and applied field dressings. Simpson smoked a cigarette meanwhile.

That, too, took time.

Then Simpson said, 'What course have you set, Colin?'

'030. Should be about right, I think.'

'Needn't be. I'd better take a sun-shot.'

'I'd rather you didn't'.

'I'm the navigator of this aircraft and I'll navigate it to Base. I'd like you to help me into the dome.'

So they lifted him into the astrodome and supported him while he sighted the sinking sun with his sextant. He calculated a correction of course, gave it to Walker, and collapsed from fatigue.

Turner, second engineer, was confronted by fuel gauges all registering zero, all broken beyond repair. What *was* the fuel situation? Despite a battle forty-five minutes long at continuous maximum power there should have been enough petrol to get them home, unless the tanks out there in the starboard wing were shot full of holes. An awful mess that wing. Looking at it from the outside made a most disturbing view. There were five tanks out there; half their fuel supplies; 100 octane. They had to know.

Turner opened the balance cocks to feed all engines from the port side, then crawled out into the thundering hot-box behind the engines on the starboard side, into the interior of the wing, a nightmarish place. Fumes in there from leaking tanks would quickly overcome him. Would anyone ever reach him? If anyone did, would they ever get him out alive? Innumerable cannon-strikes everywhere, all around him, and in the midst of them were the tanks—*intact*.

It was a shambles on the bottom deck. Walker stood and stared at it. How do you get out of this kind of thing? How do you survive? And why? How can you be shot to tatters and have only one man dead? In the turrets they were 'all right'. Not a man with a scratch. Goode was sick in the head but he'd get over that. With the others there was nothing that a sleep wouldn't fix. All over his aircraft Walker climbed and crawled and added things up, getting from place to place as best he could, circumventing jammed doors, keeping away from holes large enough to suck him out. Up in the midships turret young Fuller looked him in the eye and said, 'How about a fortnight's leave to see my little sugar-plum.'

'It's yours, boy. Make no mistake about that.'

Walker broke open the emergency rations and took orange juice to every man, calling on each man often. They could get lonely now, and scared, or sick, or terrified. No intercom to keep them in touch. Enormous reactions to cope with and overcome. Walker knew a lot about people; he had grown up in that kind of house. So round he went, keeping his crew together, giving young Jim Amiss a special grin. There he still was, hanging to that rudder bar, grey with strain, still hanging there hundreds of miles later and hours farther on.

Five hundred holes Walker counted, then gave up. Five hundred strikes, at least, on his aircraft. How *do* you survive a thing like that? Under the floorboards the hull bottom was in bits. There wouldn't be much to float with when he touched down, there wouldn't be much time on the water, she'd fill up and sink. Touch down, Colin, and leave those throttles open and charge flat-out for the beach. Or take to the dinghies and paddle to the pier. 'Here we are. We've made it, you see. All of us, except Ted. Ted's on the bomb-room floor with a blanket over his head.'

They started smashing the doors down, smashing them to pieces, to allow free movement along the lower deck, and with leak-stoppers started plugging holes below the water-line until their supplies ran out. Then they poked rags into the gaps and paper and clothing torn into strips. Was it a pointless exercise? Only time could answer that.

With an axe the engineer chopped out everything he could move. Bits of that beautiful aircraft he chopped out and threw away. Down into the sea. Wireless set, radar, mooring chain, bunks, pyrotechnics, personal possessions, empty ammunition boxes, everything that could conceivably lighten the load but not limit the capacity to fight back if the Luftwaffe returned. It was always there, that threat, the shadow of fear. They could come again. They could try another time.

There's a price on our heads until we get home.

Who puts the price there? The Germans or the law of cause and effect?

But are we not the victors? Have we not survived? Are *they* not more frightened than the Sunderland as they go flying home? Two JU 88's, alone. The complexity of their *arrival*. What are they to say? How are they to explain?

(Later we know. Secret Cannon. Armour Plate. Hull Bottom of Steel. The stories they must have told when they got home!)

Walker relieving Dowling at the controls.

Amiss still clinging to the rudder bar.

The dying day.

N/461 flying home.

Sun long gone. Twilight on the sea. Hours ticking by.

Where were they? How far had they come? How far yet to go? England must have been near, the heaven where a man could put his head down. No airspeed indicator. Rate of knots unknown. Instruments shot away. Bits of glass where instruments used to be. Just as well you carry a spare compass or two. No wireless. Silence beyond the thunder of noise. No messages in or out. No contact. No knowing if the world is still there; is England where it used to be or has it gone?

Fuller connecting up the portable dinghy radio to the aerial the Sunderland trailed behind. How long was that aerial? A hundred feet, two hundred feet? Whatever it was you unwound the reel and it drooped behind like a tail. (You forgot it sometimes and wrapped it round the waves.) Fuller wired into it and held the radio between his knees, as it was meant to be held, and turned the handle that powered the little transmitter inside. There he sat, winding, winding, as if stirring a stew, sending out an unending stream of SOSs that only the angels heard.

Land!

Every man sitting upright, every man stretching tall, and 2235 was the time. An hour and twenty-five minutes to midnight. Twilight still there. Have we made it? Are we about to arrive? Simpson dragging himself into the dome to try to identify what they saw. 'That's Cornwall.' he said, and wrote it on a slip of paper that Dowling delivered into Walker's hand.

'What are you going to do?' Dowling shouted against Walker's ear.

What *could* a man do? Too late to get to Pembroke Dock. Too far to Plymouth Sound. Get down, Colin, while you can see. Doesn't matter if it's open coast. Doesn't matter really where. Alight after dark in an aircraft like this and you'll have come this far to drown.

'I'll ditch,' Walker said, 'I'll take it in now. . . . Get everyone onto the bridge. Tell them I'll be landing close to the beach. Tell them as soon as we hit to get outside. We take to the dinghies to paddle ashore. . . . What part of Cornwall? See if he knows.'

Penzance, Simpson said. But Walker turned away and for half-an-hour more patrolled the coast up and down searching for quiet waves and a sandy beach and a state of mind. While Fuller sat in the aisle, radio between knees, winding and stirring, transmitting without pause on the international distress frequency. No one heard.

Walker then took the full weight of the controls and Amiss crawled away from the rudder bar.

'Are they ready for ditching back there?'

Dowling nodded and Walker edged close inshore. Under his wing was the village of Marazion, ahead was a stretch of beach, Prah Sands. At eight hundred feet or thereabouts he turned in along the swell, judging his speed from experience because there was nothing else to measure it by. He throttled back to make his descent and the starboard inner engine cut dead.

That was unkind.

It was not the sort of thing that should have happened; fate was pushing *too* far.

Walker turned cold, but went on down because Sunderland N would never climb again. Two engines only. No safety margin. One-shot success or one-shot disaster. Land it this time, Colin, or you'll never land again.

Slipping down until the sea was rolling in, a seven-foot sea rolling in on his nose, and there Walker flattened out and pulled all throttles off and struck the crest of a wave like lead. Into the trough he slid and pulled up wallowing, offshore by three hundred yards.

'*All out!*'

Out they went, up through the escape hatch dragging their dinghies with them, but Walker kicked open his companionway and dropped to the lower deck. Seas coming in, but not surging. Up the companionway again, shouting, '*Back inside. She's holding.*'

He opened up his engines, those two remaining engines, and at full bore charged for the shallows, wallowing and slewing and thumping and beginning to turn sluggish, beginning to sink, beginning to scrape bottom, but only two feet of water came in above the floorboards. He was as safe as the Bank of England.

Walker cut the switches and in crept silence. Sea-lapping silence.

He heaved himself from his seat and held to the back of it and regarded his crew in the crowded aisle. 'That's it,' he said. 'That'll do. That'll do us.'

Along the beach men came running—came wading into the water as Walker's men waded out of it.

'Are you safe there?' came the call. 'Do you need assistance?'

'We're all right, thank you.'

'What about your aeroplane?'

'She's had it.'

Ted Miles was coming, carried by four of his mates wading waist deep, sea surging. Up onto the beach they carried him and women with hot drinks were there to receive them, as if each night gone eleven, strange men walked up from the ocean bearing their dead, and tea on the sands was part of it.

Walker was last up, traditionally the captain's privilege, blackened and burnt and wet and filthy.

There was a house on the foreshore full of people; generous women fussing over them, hot water, clean towels, dry clothes, an enormous out-going affection, as if everybody's mother had arrived simultaneously. Where did they get the eggs from? Where did they get the sausages? Perhaps they gave the crew of N/461 the personal rations of a fortnight.

Walker asked for the telephone and shut the door behind him and rang the officers' mess, Pembroke Dock.

'Wing Commander Douglas? Can you get him for me?'

It was midnight, give or take a few minutes, and Douglas

was in the ante-room with a few of the boys drinking to the damnation of Germany.

'Douglas here. Who's speaking?'

'Col.'

'Col who?'

'Col Walker.'

'*You're dead!*'

'Not quite,' said Walker.

There is never an end. No story finishes.

In the morning the Sunderland was gone. Pieces of it, lumps of it, bits of it lay along the sands. The seas had risen and Sunderland N was only debris for the breaking.

There were decorations to come, many of them, many honours. They were feted as heroes, their fit and proper definition.

Walker did not fly again operationally. The hand fell on his shoulder and the voice said, 'I think you've had enough, son.' They sent him to Brighton, to the Australian Reception Centre, to interview arriving aircrew to determine their futures. I must have been among the first he spoke to. After the war he went to live in Canada.

Jim Amiss, like most second pilots, soon became a first pilot and was promoted to another crew. Later he became its captain. In 1971 he died in Melbourne.

Walker's crew became Bill Dowling's crew and went missing on 13 August, 1943. Nothing more was heard of them.

CHAPTER TEN

Flight by Night

John Hampshire was Commanding Officer in 1944, Dick Oldham came after him, but I had gone by then. Gone to London to write history and meet a girl.

Never did get around to charming a female while I was flying out of P.D. Took life and death and operational efficiency too seriously, I suppose, though there was a girl down town with a Welsh name living where I never knew. Wasted time, wasted year, letting her go. Was I scared of what, I'd like to know. Writing every other day to a girl back home, a beautiful girl who mystified me, neither of us ever getting through. All the friendships that never bloom.

What is time but chance and you? You live in your hour because it is there.

Captain of a Sunderland in 1944, aged 22. A century ago or last night or a future year foreseen? Did anyone ever guess how deeply seated was the fear? Or how dedicated the youth was? Or how proud? (My God, *captain* of a Sunderland: the impossible dream.) Straight as a ramrod. Skinny as a stick. Reserved. Withdrawn. Self-disciplined. Teetotal. Incredibly courteous almost all the time. Intercom on Southall's crew was like 11 a.m. on Sundays, scarcely a word out of sequence or out of tune.

They turned us into night patrols. Whether this was good or bad or wise or unwise or simply unavoidable I do not know. I never really thought the Sunderland was that kind of creature. Never looked like an owl, never felt like one. Or was that simply my bias? In the past we had taken off before dawn, patrolled all day, and landed in the evening. That was changed. Now we took off in the afternoon, patrolled all night, and landed at daybreak. Always felt topsy-turvy.

It was the year of the invasion of the continent of Europe. We trained for months in between normal operational flying. Learnt now to change our techniques. Instead of bombing by eye from deck-level as formerly, they gave us bomb-sights and electric flares and a radar homing run three hundred feet above the surface. There you were, stuck up in the heavens with the angels, pumping out flares of three hundred thousand candlepower from a chute in the tail at one-second intervals. Lighting up the ocean; lighting up yourself, dazzling everybody stupid. Here I come, Uncle Jerry; shoot me down quickly. I reckoned it was mad, reckoned they hadn't considered it, reckoned they had come up with an inventively lazy answer. Yet it worked after a fashion. Five times 461 attacked with flares in operational combat; one U-boat they sunk, the others got away slightly limping. But I swore if ever I found a U-boat which offered me the cover of darkness I would be ignoring the operational instructions that directed me to throw away the advantage. I did try once to 'put forward' my suggestion but it was dismissed as a boyish fancy. Making me, I suppose, more determined. But I practised, unobtrusively, not even my crew realizing I was doing it. I could not confide in them; I could not tell them. Orders were orders and in airforce training time you did a thing the proper way, mate, unless secretly you got more out of it than you appeared to put into it. I needed a moon, even a sliver. That was the one technological necessity—the strength and the weakness.

The invasion began.

'Good luck, chaps,' they said, but doubled the strength of the squadron to make up for the casualties. Extraordinary.

Didn't lose a man. Not for four months did a crew go missing.
  Wonderful.

It was the night of August 10/11.

Godfathers: here I sit putting it on paper and it's twenty-
nine years to the day. Rain beating over my head on a roof
of iron. Almost dark outside. Yellow light reflected on
window panes. One hundred and fifty yards from me, the
sea. Tea-tree out there, grotesquely gnarled. Traffic on the
highway; I hear the snarl. Wet paving slabs and dripping
leaves. But that is now.

I had scarcely wakened. Perhaps an hour. The night
before, we had been in the Bay. The U-boats were running
they said, coming out from the French ports in swarms.
The Allied advance on land had overrun Brittany. The U-
boat bases were under threat. The U-boats, in haste, were
leaving home, heading south or west. 'Go out there and get
them, boys.' There was some posturing at briefing time. Only
just awake again after a hard night before and someone was
hammering on the door. (I was an officer now; officers slept
in rooms; not in dormitorial lines of beds.)

"You've got to go out again, mate. I can't find your crew.
Don't you know? Haven't you heard? Every crew at P.D.
ordered into the air. The Bay's full of U-boats and no one
else can get there. Fog. Every base in England closed.' The
only time in my operational tour I was asked to patrol on
consecutive days.

The crew was found in a couple of hours; they were not
far, but our aircraft was four hundred miles away. Someone
else had jumped into it and gone hunting down the Bay.
'You can have P/Peter,' they said, 'We're knocking her into
shape now. Treat her gently though. She's been having a
major overhaul and is not exactly *finished*, you know.'

Should have been P for Priscilla. No Sunderland ever was
male.

They were still swarming over her when we went aboard.

154

This was unserviceable. *That* was unserviceable. 'We're working on her, sir. We'll have her right. Never fear.' Take-off, I think, was 2200 hours. Maintenance men were still running up and down stairs three minutes to starting time.

But up she went and away we flew, everyone aboard trying to get used to things that were strange. You become accustomed to your own machine. Z was ours. No doubt somebody owned P but no one had flown it for such a time that it wasn't like *anyone's* aeroplane. (Flew it often after that; ended up liking it more than our own.) Got her up to five hundred feet, everything looking fine, switched on the radar and nothing showed.

'Are you sure?'

'Dead as the dodo, Captain. A blank screen.'

A night patrol without S.E. was like a day patrol without engines. You'd have been better to have stayed at home.

Too much rush. Too much pressure. Sending us off without our secret equipment; that was bad. Yet how could we go home? 'You've got to get there,' they said at briefing. 'The main thing is being there, keeping those U-boats down, until the fog over England clears.' There we'd be, on our own. Any other night half-a-dozen aircraft or more would have covered the same plot flying parallel patrols.

So what do you do?

Swear?

All this fuss and fury to get into the air for no purpose you would ever *see*. Your radar was your sight by night: without it you were blind. So off you'd go patrolling with U-boats underneath in ranks of three and you'd never know.

Would you care?

If you don't attack, you don't get shot down.

If you fly the other way you live to fly another day.

That's not as stupid as it sounds.

I resent this business of having to fly not properly prepared. I don't like haste where these things are concerned.

An operational flight is a state of mind. It begins many
hours before, even a day or more before. Because when you
are to fly, you know. It's your *turn*. Flying out of turn is like
flying in someone's else's clothes with the wrong things in the
pockets, the wrong photographs, the wrong New Testament,
the wrong cigarette case. The wrong things are no *good* for
you. They don't *work* for you. It's even the wrong aeroplane.

'Stevenson to Captain.'

Keith Stevenson, straight air gunner. What was he doing
on the intercom so soon?

'I'd like to have a go at the radar. I'd like a chance to fix
it.'

Well, if anyone could, Stevenson could. He had a feeling
for radar, not officially approved. One did not entrust
equipment of that kind to straight air gunners (said the
masters of our lives), only to pilots and wireless operators
and technicians of the more intelligent breeds. But Stevenson
had broken the rules. He was better at the game than the
experts. His idea of a riotous afternoon was to creep un-
observed into the radar workshop at P.D. and *spy*. They
never shot him, but it's a wonder. There might have been
another crew member of 461 with his peculiar and specialized
knowledge, but I doubt it. Aircrew didn't *fiddle* with radar:
in behind those secret grey boxes were vast complexities
and dangerous voltages.

'Captain to Stevenson. Go ahead.'

He had a screwdriver and a lead pencil. That was what
he worked with. The man was mad. He worked in the dark.
He was crazy. His screwdriver wasn't insulated. Fellows off
watch stood round gaping at him. Taking things to bits and
testing them. Putting them back different ways and experi-
menting. While P flew on to the Bay of Biscay.

I knew we were going somewhere. That is not the wisdom
of later reflection. It is given fancy names these days like
Extra Sensory Perception. Back in 1944 it was an itch, a
worry, a certainty. You don't get pulled out of bed when you

don't expect it for nothing. You get pulled out of bed for a purpose. There's a job to do or the wheel has stopped turning. Is it curtains?

Two and a half hours out of Pembroke Dock the intercom switches on and someone is saying, 'Stevenson to Captain. Radar serviceable.'

So Keith S. gets Mentioned in Despatches.

In another hour we are a few miles west of Brest heading deeply into the inner Bay on a course of 165 compass. Half-past one in the morning. No fog anywhere that we can see. An intensely black sky with hard bright stars and pale blue flames in our exhausts. As if the entire universe and you have been created solely for each other. (As that night perhaps they were.) There is no one else around. The whole inner Bay is ours until dawn. Imagine what it means. If U-boats are there and we fail to see them they get through. We take that very seriously. Yet I am not *happy* with the patrol. I should not be there at all. I am out of sequence.

'Tail to Control. There are lights in the sky astern.'

(That was a most odd thing to say.)

'What do you mean?'

'You'd better look.'

Ossie Pederick is Control.

'I don't know,' he says. 'Captain —?'

Not surprising he doesn't know. No one else knows either. What do you do with a sky full of lights? We can't even count them. Red lights. Yellow lights. Faint lights. Bright lights. Some at immense (incalculable) heights? Some at sea level. Some in patterns. Some at random. *And no radar indication of any kind.*

'Captain to Tail. Where did they come from?'

'They appeared.'

'You've lots of experience, Bob. Have you seen anything like them?'

'Never.'

'Are they getting closer?'

'I don't know.' A tone to his voice as if worried, as if perplexed. Bob Hobbs, our Cockney air gunner.

We go on watching them. They go on staying there, constantly moving, constantly changing position, always astern an unknown distance off. Might have been five miles. Might have been fifty. No air raids that night. Aircraft fog-bound. No bombers passing.

I don't know. I didn't then. I still don't.

Omens. Omens.

Group calls us with a message. '*Emergency. Total surface bombing restriction.*'

Pederick plots the position and places it marginally east of the southern limit of our patrol. Must be an Allied submarine. What other explanation?

'What time do we get there, Control?'

'0230.'

At 0153 up comes the moon, half visible, half in the earth's shadow, edging through surface cloud, laying down a beam five degrees wide. That's the sort of thing I notice; width of beam, brilliance of beam, in the event of the miracle happening and up popping a U-boat. But it's *got* to be a half-baked notion. You do it as they train you. You perform like a mouse on a treadwheel. That is why they train you. To avoid the need under stress of working out the technicalities. So that you react from instinct. So that all the intelligence not stifled by panic you can apply to the unexpected. Though it is *extraordinary* how rarely the unexpected happens. Disciplined men on both sides react predictably. If they are trained with stupidity they react as stupidly as stupid can be. So you sit there, thinking.

'Tail to Control. The lights! They've gone! As if someone had clicked a switch. Not a sign of them.'

Omens. Every man aboard left slightly edgy.

'S.E. to Control. I have a contact. Five degrees port. Eighteen miles.'

That's interesting.

'S.E. to Control. It's showing I.F.F.'

Meaning *Identification Friend or Foe*, a reassuring little blip pulsing at three-second intervals.

'S.E. to Control. Still five degrees port. Now fifteen miles. Breaking up into several contacts.'

'Control to Captain. The Second Escort Group is in the vicinity.'

So we are not alone entirely. There sweeps the Royal Navy keeping each other company. How many men? More than a thousand? Do they know what it's like high in the heavens, each airman alone on his own little island? Does it matter if they don't? Do they have to?

Sunderland in the sky. Invisible.

Southall and Player and Wylie and Pederick and Eshelby and Rintoul and Wyeth and Norris and Kendall and Hobbs and Stevenson each on his own little island.

Ships on the moon-ray silhouetted for an instant. There they are. See them. Five sharp ships in a cold white slit at 0218 in the morning, a chink in a door of blackness. And they don't even shoot at us.

Change of watch on the radar. Half-an-hour of that kind of eye-strain is all that's wise for anyone.

Still flying east of south, still on 165 compass, still at a thousand feet, still sitting there adding up the omens.

'S.E. to Control.' Sounds like Norris. 'Radar contact ten degrees port. Ten miles. No I.F.F. showing.'

It had to happen, so it happens.

And Bobby Norris tells you.

All the way down into the Bay it's been getting ready for the meeting. No surprise in Southall. No introductions necessary.

'S.E. to Control. Contact is on the surface. Fifteen degrees port. Nine miles. No I.F.F. showing.'

Like listening to a news bulletin with your name in it. You know all about it before you hear it.

A man can say these things now. He can write them. And accept them.

You sit there on the bridge of your Sunderland functioning not normally. Luminous instrument faces vaguely before you. Your thinking is neither broad nor incisive. It is rudimentary.... There is something here I must rise to cope with; that's the sort of thing your brain keeps telling you. I am at the brink of combat. Life has reached a climax. Is it too big for me? I am about to kill or be killed or reveal myself as a coward. It's an awful, awful responsibility. . . .

All those lives in your hands, all those intangibles, all the loving and the healing, all those pasts and presents and futures. (Drop a depth-charge here, hit or miss, and you shake the planet.) Disgrace yourself and you shame your family. Kill and will you ever forget it? Here you are, three-parts pacifist, a peaceful young man, never thrown a fist in anger or had a serious argument, now with a vibrating control column in your hands and the firing button for four fixed machine-guns under one thumb and the firing button for eight depth-charges under the other thumb and an innate ability to aim by eye without instruments at practice targets and scarcely ever miss them. A numbness grows. You are long past accepting the certainty even though no one else seems to realize it. Only thirty seconds have passed since Norris last switched off his microphone.

He switches on again. 'S.E. to Control. Twenty degrees port. Eight miles. I.F.F. still not showing.'

Pulse racing. Limbs trembling. Already breathing through an open mouth deeply. Yet the numbness goes on spreading as if coursing through the bloodstream; half of me goes on panicking, half is under an anaesthetic. Climax and decision are imminent.

That moonbeam. There it lies like a side-attachment to the aircraft. There it moves with us over the water. Into it comes the ship as expected, long and lean and low, steaming southward. Life inside me somehow stopping.

'Second Pilot to Captain. There's a wake in the moonbeam. A ship of some sort. Peculiar looking.'

'Captain to Control, I see it. We're too high. I'm turning away from it.' Why say *too high*? Why give it away before I'm ready.

So I go to starboard and the gunner in midships calls me. 'Midships to Captain. I see it. Never seen anything like it.'

'Thank you. Keep your eye on it. . . . Captain to S.E. Continue with bearings and distances.'

The first pilot is moving into the seat beside me. Reg Player. Second Pilot Wylie has vacated.

"S.E. to Captain, Contact five miles. Dead astern.'

'Control to Captain. It's on the fringe of the bombing-restriction area.'

'How close to the fringe?'

'Very close.'

Player is leaning across and shouting. 'Is it a U-boat?'

'Yes.'

'S.E. to Captain. Six miles. Dead astern.'

Player shouting again. 'How are you going to attack?'

'Up-moon. No flares.'

But I fly farther away in a zone of confusion and indecision and rampantly running fear; the natural part of me making its last stand, delaying the climax, squeezing a few extra seconds out of life *because I do not know |the outcome.* My sensitivity does not reach that far. I have foreseen the U-boat. I have foreseen the attack. But the end I cannot see. I fear that the end is the end. I fear I am about to die by self-imposed decision.

'S.E. to Captain. Seven miles. Dead astern.'

Player is shouting again. 'You're going the wrong way.'

Of course I'm going the wrong way because I'm not yet ready to go the right way. But everybody knows by now it is a submarine and everybody knows the captain is flying in the wrong direction. Everybody also knows there is a terrible problem.

'Navigator to Captain.' Ossie Pederick dropping his title, not calling himself *Control* (another omen?), framing the terrible question: 'Do you think it's British?'

'I don't know.'

But I do know. I have no doubt. I know it is not British. I know it has been waiting through every day of my life, from birth to this instant. (*I am a coward; I am running away; I also know that.*)

'S.E. to Captain. Eight miles. Dead astern.'

But the klaxon is sounding with my finger on it. A blind and hopeless act of defiance. I sound the horn. I hear it. I've done it. I'm committed.

'Captain to S.E. I'm turning. I will be trying to get the target on the moonpath.'

'Navigator to Captain. Do you want me to go down to the bomb-sight?'

'Please.'

'Engineer to Captain. Standing by in the bomb-bay.'

'Thank you.'

'Second Pilot to Captain. Do you want R/T for the Escort Group?'

'Please.'

'Flare-chute to Captain. In position.'

'Thank you.'

Turning very steeply onto a reciprocal course, nose depressed, trying to reduce height, but I must have too much power because I go up rather than down. The moon comes round, dead ahead. There lies the moonbeam. No U-boat.

'S.E. to Captain. No contact, Can't find it.'

A roaring sound overwhelms me, like a train in a tunnel, all but deafening. *What the hell is it?* The R/T, the spoken language link with the Naval Escort Group, has gone wild. I scream. "SWITCH THAT THING OFF.' But no one hears. No one *can* hear. It is an incredible, crushing, nerve-destroying clamour. I can't think. I scream into the blackness of the bridge: "SWITCH IT OFF. SWITCH IT OFF.' But I seem to be alone. Everyone has gone aft, behind the black-out curtain. I can't see them. They can't see me.

There is no communication. I can't give orders. I can't find the U-boat. 'SWITCH IT OFF.'

Shattering silence. My head goes on spinning.

'W/T to Captain. I don't know what that was. I'll look into it later.'

'S.E. to Captain. I have the contact. Eight miles. Thirty degrees port.'

What is it doing round there?

Should be on the moonbeam!

Player returns to the right-hand seat, having silenced the noise, and I'm wanting badly to pick up that U-boat, quickly ⸢and efficiently, to relieve Player's reasonable anxieties. This is not the way to conduct a U-boat attack and everyone knows it.

So I go hunting that U-boat, turning port to find it, watching my moonbeam which is no longer cooperative. It won't stay where I want it. It has a will of its own.

If I don't get it soon I'll lose it.

'Captain to Engineer. I'm running out the bombs.'

'S.E. to Captain. Eight miles. Thirty degrees starboard.'

That was impossible.

'Engineer to Captain. Bomb doors have jammed. The racks have not extended.'

All right, mate. Take it calmly. If the bomb doors have jammed, they've jammed. If the contact's thirty degrees starboard it's thirty degrees starboard . . .

'Captain to S.E. I'm turning . . . Captain to Engineer. Try force on the bomb doors. All the muscle you can call on.'

Sliding across the moonpath. No sign of the U-boat.

'Captain to Turrets. Keep a sharp look-out. If it's on the radar, it must be on the surface. We've *got* to see it. I'm turning. I'll fly an S course, back and forth, until we get it. Where is it, S.E.?'

'Well round to starboard. Seven and a half miles.'

'Engineer to Captain. Bomb doors open. Bombs are out.'

Beside me the indicator lights are shining. I select six switches and fuse them.

'Thank you, Engineer.'

'Midships to Captain!' Explosively. 'On the moonpath now.'

Aileron and rudder jammed on, violently turning. Midships might have seen it, but for me there's not a glimpse. Are those fellows wondering what I'm doing? They must be. I've never talked moonpath to them. They haven't a clue what I'm at. And who'd blame them?

How long is it since we started this lark? Incredibly, only a couple of minutes. Time has nothing to do with the face of the clock. Where's that U-boat?

Weaving back and forth, widely, across the moonpath.

'S.E. to Captain. Six and three-quarter miles. Five degrees starboard.'

So close!

Easy. . . . Easy. . . . Degree by degree edging onto the moon. . . . Mustn't lose it this time. This is the last time. This is the only time.

There.

Black and sharp and stark.

A perfect silhouette.

'S.E. to Captain, Dead ahead. Six miles.'

'You can say that again, Bobby! You can stop reporting. Target visible.'

Fine. Now they can sit back and watch. Now, little by little, they're going to learn what this is all about. And so am I. It's still a theory. I say I have unlimited visibility up moon. I say the enemy cannot see me down moon. I say I can make an attack as in daylight. I say I will achieve complete visual surprise unless they plot me by radar as first we plotted them. And if I bumble this unrehearsed attack there will be hell to pay when I get back to base, if I get back to base. 'Who do you think you are? Devising your own tactics. You have a laid-down procedure. You have bomb-sight and flares and a crew superbly trained to use them.'

There is a troublesome tremble in arms and legs and spine. No rigidity at the kneecaps. It's a long, smooth dive. A long, smooth, deliberate approach. I have turned a U-boat into a practice target. Why fight like heroes when wit hurts less? But I have not dived at high power towards the sea at night before. No one knows that. But it does not scare me.

Five miles.

'Second Pilot to Captain. Colour of the hour is red.'

It looks like a toy. Still on its southerly heading, cruising at eight or nine knots. How can it not know we are here? There will be four men or five in the conning-tower searching with night glasses. There will be a radar-search-receiver. and we are thundering in the heavens like Thor.

'Navigator to Captain. Do you want me to use the bomb-sight?'

'No, I'm bombing by eye.'

'Flare-chute to Captain. At what range do you want your flares.'

'No range. No flares. I'm using the moon.'

Four miles.

'Captain to W/T. Send your flash report now. I want it away before we attack.'

'W/T understood.'

Down to five hundred feet. That's where I'll stay. I'll be needing height for evasive action. Once they get my bearing, once they get my range, I'll be throwing this aircraft every-where.

Three miles.

Airspeed creeping up to a hundred and sixty knots. Reg Player gives me more power. I set the four fixed guns at fire—that new armament they have given us to sweep U-boat decks clean, four extra Brownings, thousands of extra rounds per minute. Here I am, that quiet young man, setting myself up, bunching at the controls, thumb on gun-button, thumb on bomb release, as taut as violins.

'Captain to Nose. Who's there?'

'Stevenson.'

'Keith, will you not fire unless they shoot first. I repeat do not fire.'

Two miles.

Flying in straight and level at a hundred and sixty knots. Five hundred feet. Filling the air waves with radar and wireless transmissions, blue flames streaming from our exhausts, engines thunderously roaring.

The submarine maintaining course and speed, no action visible on deck through the binoculars, no apparent awareness of Sunderland P/Peter.

It is unnatural.

I have to lose height. I cannot stay up here any longer.

Stabbing at the rudder constantly. Holding the target central in the moonbeam, instinctively allowing for courses and speeds, ready for instant evasion, mind going dull again, going stupid again, an enormous nerve-tremble gathering.

One mile.

Nose down. Get your height off. You're far too high for bombing.

Where's the flak? Why aren't they firing? Where's the flak I should be evading?

I can see the guns. Are they not manning them?

Half-a-mile.

Too high. Nose down positively. Diving steeply. Moon-beam on the water. Moon standing high on the windscreen. Target heading south at eight knots unvaryingly.

They'll cut me to pieces. They'll blast me to fragments at the last instant. They're sitting on their sights. They've got to be.

Five hundred yards.

Life expectancy zero. A vast nerve tremble.

No flak coming.

Diving almost vertically for the water.

There are seamen on the bridge. Four of them. White faces in the moonlight. Upturned faces in the moonlight.

DEPTH-CHARGE THEM.
'BOMBS GONE.'
Conning-tower directly underneath me. Only feet and inches in it. Stick dragged back, squashing over the top of them, plunging out of the moonbeam into blackness.
"Midships to Captain. It fired a red flare.'
'Tail to Captain. Flak.'
Undulating, with tracer streams trailing behind me and suddenly, overwhelmingly, an emotional sickness. Every thing has succeeded superbly.
No more flak. All is darkness. Can't even see the moon-beam. No longer interested in it. It's astern, I think. I've turned through a hundred and eighty degrees or some-thing like it. The target should be on the port side about a thousand yards from me.
'Engineer to Captain. I watched from the galley. You straddled it. Two depth-charges to starboard. Four to port. When they went up I couldn't see it for foam and flame. It was a blue-white flash.'
'What about the flare?'
'Yes, I saw that. It was red.'
'Captain to S.E. Do you still have the contact?'
'Yes.'
'So it hasn't sunk yet.'
There is a yellow flame on the sea; our marine marker burning, dropped with the depth-charges. From beside the flame six streams of coloured tracer shells erupt.
'Captain to Turrets. Do not return the fire.'
It scorches away behind us, too high and off direction.
'First Pilot to Captain. I've checked the colours. Red is right for the hour.'
'Thank you.'
'Are you going round for another attack?'
'No.'
I am still sick.
If I have attacked a British submarine what do I do?

If I am in the course of sinking a British submarine how do I take off the crew? Or are they dead already? Why was I so certain it was my right and proper target? Is this the end I was unable to foresee?

Pederick comes up from below, from the bomb-sight. Comes up the companionway and puts a hand on my shoulder and shouts in my ear, 'I'll take a fix on Gee.'

Gee. A radio-navigational aid. A new tool to help us in the Bay; help we need now. If we are in the bombing-restriction area what shape will the world take for me—the dark new world to begin perhaps moments from now?

It is the responsibility of the submarine to identify itself in the presence of aircraft, just as it is the responsibility of aircraft to identify in the presence of naval surface ships. This is why we have pyrotechnic cartridges and Verey pistols and regularly changing colours. But if you achieve complete surprise, if you stalk a submarine and beat it hands down and it has no opportunity to identify . . .?

'Captain to W/T. Send off the first sighting report. Report to read: "Submarine was on surface. Fought back. Course and speed two hundred and twenty degrees, eight knots. Sighted at eight miles".'

The first pilot's eyes are looking my way. Is it by the moon that I see them? Whites of eyes. What is the crew thinking? Each man; what does he feel? *Relief* that he did not personally press the button or fire the guns? The captain performed the deed.

'Navigator to Captain. The Gee-fix places our present position at fifteen miles from the bombing-restriction area.'

I find myself nodding but not dancing round the cockpit. It is a reassurance but there are too many unknowns. There is the enormity of the red flare. The most crushing enormity of my conscious years.

'S.E. to Captain. The contact has disappeared.'

Has it submerged? Is the sea littered with bodies? Are

dinghies everywhere? Those little one-man dinghies that bloom over the grave like flowers after submarines die?

Do you rejoice? Do you blow out your brains?

'Captain to Flare-chute operator. I will make a homing run on the marine marker. I want you to illuminate at half a mile. Captain to all positions. A sharp watch please.'

So we fly in and light up the sea. No dinghies. No wreckage. No bodies. No oil, Just the marine marker burning curiously as if nothing had occurred.

'Captain to Control. Do I have R/T?'

'Yes. The trouble is cured.'

I switch through and call the Escort Group, using the call-sign with which one must open proceedings. 'Hullo, Turret. This is Shameless Peter. Shameless Peter calling Turret. How do you receive me? Over.'

They are north of us at ten miles. That we read off the radar screen. Have they seen the flak or the flares? Are they already steaming south as fast as they can go? Back comes the reply: 'Hullo, Shameless Peter. This is Matapan. Receiving you loud and clear. Over.'

(The Second Escort Group, as we had known, but protocol must be observed.)

'Shameless Peter to Matapan. Receiving you also loud and clear. Message for you.'

'Pass your message.'

'We have attacked a submarine bearing from you two hundred and thirty degrees True. We estimate a straddle with six weapons. It has submerged in that position. We have dropped a marine marker. Is this understood? Over.'

'Message understood. We saw the tracer fire. Please repeat bearing.'

'Two hundred and thirty degrees True. Ten miles. We will fly over you with navigation lights burning heading for the marine marker.'

Why do I say that? Navigation lights *burning*? Am I hoping to be shot down? Am I saying to fate, take the equalizer? Or is it an overwhelming urge to placate fate, to push everything over the edge? I think I am saying: 'This has been too easy. I must take a major risk. I must show I am prepared to accept what I give.'

(No one ever picked me up on it. I threw it down and it was ignored. No one ever commented. No one ever asked, 'Navigational lights in an operational area? *Why?*' And no one shot me down.)

There I sit, waiting for the Navy to call, waiting sick, waiting for them to say: 'You have attacked a British submarine.'

The waiting is *endless*. I think I am waiting hours later, even days later waiting for everything to be turned upside down. Even after I know it is a U-boat and there can be no doubt in the whole wide world I am still waiting for fate to reverse the tale.

The Navy says nothing. The voice doesn't call.

We turn north of the ships and fly south directly over them towards the marine marker distantly burning, adding our light to the stars and the moon. Green light, red light, white light; we twinkle in the sky.

No comment from the Navy. No call.

What was that bombing-restriction zone for?

Who put it there? Why? Was the devil abroad? Who sent it into the air? Was he British or German or clown? We never learn.

For hours we circle, twinkling in the black sky. Up comes U-385 at dawn, wallowing, unable to steer, unable to manoeuvre, rudder gone, starboard-after hydroplane torn off, starboard screw shattered, air unbreathable, water pouring inward; up it came ten minutes after we had gone. Naval gunfire on the sea. Forty-one German submariners in their little dinghies when their ship went down. Forty-one prisoners for the Navy to take home. Twenty-nine years ago as I write.

The ghosts in a man's past. They do not walk each day with him but once in a while they come for the remembering. Once in a while a flying log book falls open. But never a nightmare, not now; there must be some kind of inbuilt defence. One must not question it in case the defence breaks down.

So I have taken you into a squadron and now take you out of it. The squadron was there before me and remained after I had gone. But I had had enough at the end. They did not ask me to do eight hundred hours. Four months more and I had taken all I could stand. My voice was fraught with tensions on the intercom; it broke on the R/T one day in a storm on the harbour at P.D.

John Hampshire said, 'I think you've had enough; don't you?' He did it kindly. He did it well. 'Where would you like to go? What would you like to do?'

I went to London and wrote the history of the squadron that was then my life. And met a girl who became my wife. And lived for two years in that most exciting of all cities. Long ago.

GLOSSARY

AILERONS: Panels in the trailing edges of the wings which move up and down in immediate response to the pilot's control column, causing the wing to rise or fall. Used in association with the rudder to turn left or right.

ASDIC: A device which listens to sounds and measures the distance and direction between itself and the source of the sound.

BANK: The angle the wings assume during a manoeuvre or turn.

BOLLARD: A strong metal 'knob' or anchorage to which mooring ropes and cables are fastened.

BOOM: Man-made obstruction at harbour mouth to prevent entry of enemy vessels.

BOX BARRAGE: Many shells from a number of guns fired simultaneously to form in the air a densely-packed pattern of explosives.

BULKHEAD: An internal wall, usually with a door through it Similar to the compartmental partitions in a railway carriage.

CORDITE: A type of explosive with a distinctive 'gun-powder' smell.

COWLINGS: The engine covers—similar in function to the bonnet or hood of a motor car.

ELEVATORS: Panels in the trailing edges of the tailplane which move up and down in immediate response to the pilot's control column, causing the aircraft to climb or descend.

FREE FRENCH: After the defeat of France: French nationals based outside France fighting on against Germany and Italy (and subsequently Japan) in the name of France. Led by General Charles de Gaulle.

Glossary

GROUP: In this book referring to No 19 Group Headquarters R.A.F. Coastal Command, at Plymouth in the south of England.

PINNACE: A large, often handsome, and useful motor launch with a crew of up to three or four, used for towing flying-boats, for air-sea-rescue, for ferrying aircrew from place to place, and for harbour duties.

R/T: Abbreviation for Radio Telegraphy; at the time of this story a method of direct voice communication over short distances between two or more radio transmitter/receivers tuned to the same wavelength.

SAINT ELMO'S FIRE: A harmless natural phenomenon; a continuous electrical discharge occurring in thundery conditions, visible on projecting parts of an aircraft usually as a blue glow.

SEAR: A movable catch in the gun-lock mechanism which prevents the gun from firing.

STRINGER: Part of the aircraft's *skeleton*—a structural member of the airframe.

RACER: A burning bullet or shell visible in flight. Used as an aid for aiming.

TRIM: A well 'trimmed' aircraft is easier to fly than a badly trimmed aircraft. Trim is adjusted by changing the angle at which small movable panels, called trimming-tabs, meet the air during flight. These tabs are usually adjacent to the major control surfaces—that is, the ailerons, elevators and rudder. They respond only to deliberate mechanical adjustment.

TURRET: A 'rotating' transparent gun-platform, usually dome-shaped, which allows good visibility to the gunner who sits inside it. Hydraulic controls, operated by the gunner, enable the gunner to turn the turret quickly to face any direction within the traverse of the turret, the traverse being the total distance it may swing from side to side.

Glossary

W/T: Abbreviation for Wireless Telegraphy; at the time of this story a method of direct communication by Morse Code between two or more short-wave (i.e., long-distance) wireless transmitter/receivers tuned to the same wavelength.

TYPICAL U-BOAT

Front Deck

Anchor

Torpedo Tubes